PYRAMID

PYRAMID

BEYOND IMAGINATION

INSIDE THE GREAT PYRAMID OF GIZA

Kevin Jackson
and Jonathan Stamp

Published to accompany the television programme
Pyramid, first broadcast on BBC1 in 2002.
Producer: Jonathan Stamp
Computer graphics produced by MillTv, London.

First published 2002
© Kevin Jackson and Jonathan Stamp
The moral right of the authors has been asserted.

ISBN 0 563 48803 4

Published by BBC Worldwide Ltd,
Woodlands, 80 Wood Lane, London W12 0TT

Commissioning editor: Shirley Patton
Project editor: Christopher Tinker
Copy-editor: Esther Jagger
Art director: Linda Blakemore
Designer: Paul Vater at Sugar Free
Picture researcher: Deirdre O'Day
Proofreader: Christine King

Set in Foundry Old Style
Printed and bound in Great Britain by Butler & Tanner Ltd, Frome
Colour separations by Radstock Reproductions Ltd, Midsomer Norton
Jacket printed by Lawrence-Allen Ltd, Weston-super-Mare

CONTENTS

WONDERFUL
THINGS

THE LAST SURVIVING WONDER

THE PEOPLE OF CLASSICAL TIMES knew that many things were marvellous, but saw that only a few of these things were the work of humanity rather than of the gods. And of these miracles of human ingenuity, only a very few were deemed worthy of universal admiration. You could number them on the fingers of two hands. They were: the Hanging Gardens of Babylon; the Temple of Artemis at Ephesus; the giant statue of Zeus at Olympia – the work of Athens's greatest sculptor, Phidias (*c.* 490– *c.* 415 BC), also renowned for creating the heroic marble forms for the façade of the Parthenon, works now known to the British as the Elgin Marbles; the Pharos, or lighthouse-fortress, of Alexandria, built in 279 BC to the designs of Sostratus, an Asiatic Greek in the service of the Ptolemies, and dedicated to 'the Saviour Gods' – an edifice well over 400 feet (122 metres) high, and topped by a mirror-like structure which combined the functions of reflector

The Great Pyramid, one of the Seven Wonders of the World, as depicted in a seventeenth-century engraving.

and telescope. Then there were the Colossus of Rhodes – a bronze statue of the sun-god Helios, which towered over the entrance to Rhodes harbour and was reported by the elder Pliny to be some 70 cubits (100 feet / 30 metres) tall; and the Mausoleum at Halicarnassus – a white marble tomb for Mausolus, ruler of Caria (377–353 BC), well over 130 feet (40 metres) high, erected by his widow Artemisia and decorated with carvings by the brilliant sculptor Scopas. Finally, there was the Great Pyramid of Cheops (also known as Khufu), at Giza.

These were the Seven Wonders of the Ancient World, as compiled by the Greek poet Antipator of Sidon around 130 BC. Scholars and adventurers undertook long and arduous journeys to visit them, then came home again and told or wrote awe-inspiring tales of what they had seen. The Seven Wonders passed into legend.

Centuries passed, and time took its usual revenge on these monuments of vaulting ambition. An earthquake toppled the Colossus of Rhodes in 224 BC. The Pharos survived almost a millennium longer, and was still in use after the Arab conquest of Egypt, but was itself destroyed by earthquakes in AD 700. Earthquakes also did away with the Mausoleum in the fifteenth century AD. Of Phidias's great Olympian Zeus, visited by Pausanias and described in his epic ten-volume travel book, the *Guide to Greece*, nothing is left except a tiny image on the coins of Elis. Almost all the Wonders were destroyed: the sands rose and buried them, or – when a few recognizable ruins survived – the thieves came looting, while rats bred and scurried among the rubble.

Eventually, however, starting with a slow trickle of interest in the early Renaissance and building into a flood in the nineteenth and twentieth centuries, new bands of travellers from younger countries came to follow in the path of the classical wanderers, and thrilled to their gradual rediscovery of the grand archaic ruins. This time, however, they came with a very different frame of mind. They looked, not on perfected structures, but on shards and fragments; they reflected, not on the splendours of human achievement, but on its transience. If the great nations of Egypt, Greece and Babylon had fallen, how long could, say, Germany or France or Spain hope to thrive? A thousand years? Five hundred? Less?

Percy Bysshe Shelley. His poem 'Ozymandias' was based on a traveller's tale from ancient Egypt recorded by Diodorus.

The reflective mood was caught most memorably near the start of the nineteenth century by the English poet Shelley, who was fascinated to discover that some ancient writers had anticipated this very modern spirit. He found a traveller's tale from ancient Egypt recorded in the pages of the historian Diodorus Siculus, who wrote in Greek. The story, already a couple of centuries old when Diodorus wrote it down some time around 49 BC, told of one Hectaeus of Abdera, a contemporary of Alexander the Great who journeyed throughout Egypt and recorded his impressions.

One day, Hectaeus came across the ruins of what had been built by one of the most powerful of all the pharaohs, Ramesses II, believed by some to be the pharaoh mentioned in the Old Testament book of Exodus. In Greek, Ramesses's throne name was rendered as *user-maat-re*, or 'strong in right is Re'. Shelley seized on this word, anglicized it, and turned it into 'Ozymandias':

> I met a traveller from an antique land
> Who said: Two vast and trunkless legs of stone
> Stand in the desert. Near them on the sand,
> Half sunk, a shattered visage lies, whose frown

And wrinkled lip and sneer of cold command
Tell that its sculptor well those passions read
Which yet survive, stamped on these lifeless things,
The hand that mocked them and the heart that fed.
And on the pedestal these words appear:

'My name is Ozymandias, King of Kings:
Look on my works, ye mighty, and despair!'
Nothing beside remains. Round the decay
Of that colossal wreck, boundless and bare,
The lone and level sands stretch far away.

The sombre ironies and implicit threat to tyrants of the modern age – for Shelley was a revolutionary – helped make the poem one of the most famous short verses in the English language. Schoolchildren were made to learn it by heart, though not, perhaps, to enquire too deeply into its politics. It is a remarkable poem, and yet the truth it tells is only a partial one. For if the Ramesseum and the other magnificent wrecks of Egypt's golden age reminded visitors that *sic transit gloria mundi* – 'so passes the glory of the world' – there was one monument which told exactly the opposite story: a story of triumph over time.

Six of the Seven Wonders vanished. The seventh endured, to be called by various names: the Pyramid of Giza; Khufu's Pyramid; most commonly and justly of all, the Great Pyramid. Four and a half thousand years after its creation, the Pyramid still stands, still strikes awe into everyone who sees it. True, it has suffered some damage – the glorious white limestone casing which once made it gleam and dazzle in the Egyptian sunlight has long since been stripped off; builders have helped themselves to some of its stones for their own, more modest creations; and it has been centuries since grave-robbers looted its magnificent interior.

Still, it endures: the greatest time traveller of all. Awesome, of course, in its sheer scale, and in the thought of the human effort that went into its making, but awesome in its other qualities, too. Awesome in the astonishing accuracy of its proportions – an architectural feat to rival anything that can be done with steel and glass and concrete by modern builders armed with computers, and all performed by a race whose main tools of measurement were the rope and the stick. Awesome in its dazzlingly precise alignment with north, and in its complex relationship with the sun, moon and stars – features which modern archaeologists and astronomers are only now, at the beginning of the twenty-first century, beginning to comprehend. Awesome, above all, in its mystery. What does the building mean? What motive could possibly have been powerful enough to compel the expenditure of so much labour, skill, ingenuity and treasure on a structure with no apparent function? Who were the people who built such a marvel, and how – how on earth – did they accomplish it?

It is no surprise that the Pyramid should have inspired wild answers to these difficult questions. That vast and enigmatic form, known to almost everyone on earth, has been the object of speculation that ranges from the contentious via the merely fanciful to the frankly insane. The steady output of writings on the subject since the twelfth century AD became an entire publishing industry by the end of the nineteenth century, as a motley army of mystics, theosophists, spiritualists, charlatans and conspiracy-mongers set themselves up to reveal the (supposed) Secret of the Pyramid.

Among the more celebrated contenders in the field were those who insisted that the Pyramid was built with the use of esoteric magic – an occult tradition then passed down from the Egyptian priesthood via Hermes Trismegistus (see page 121) to ... well, whoever had written the book you were reading. Then there were those who believed that the Pyramid's famously intricate dimensions were a coded account of – among other ludicrous claims – the rise of the Nazis, or the French Revolution, or the entire course of history from creation to (imminent) Armageddon. It did not escape the attention of conspiracy theorists that the US dollar bill bears the image of a pyramid.

As popular madnesses developed, pyramid theories evolved along with them. In the 1960s and 1970s devotees of New Age wisdom, noting how well the Egyptians managed to preserve their dead in these structures, claimed that little plastic pyramid models could be used around the house to keep milk fresh, razor blades sharp, plants blooming and what have you. And those with an extra-terrestrial bent were fond of claiming that the Great Pyramid – manifestly too extraordinary a creation to be the work of unaided humanity – was inspired (or, as the extremists would have it, even built) by helpful teams of passing aliens: possibly from Sirius, one of the stars with which Khufu's building does indeed have a demonstrable link.

Before photography enabled people around the world to see for themselves what the Giza plateau really looked like, there had been a tendency for artists to romanticize it. In his famous watercolour of 1848, *Approach of the Simoon*, for example, the English painter David Roberts has the Sphinx, which actually faces east, facing west.

All of which was, in a sense, harmless nonsense. In another sense, it was pernicious nonsense, since it sent thousands of readers haring off after imaginary secrets and splendours when a whole set of real, verifiable and fascinating secrets and splendours were there for the investigating.

This book, although it will look from time to time at some of the crazier things that have been believed about the Great Pyramid, will stay strictly in the realms of demonstrable fact or well-justified conjecture, in the belief that the truth is ultimately more enthralling, and even more inspiring, than the most lurid of those wild apocryphal theories. To try to justify this claim right from the outset, let us consider a little more closely the most immediately overwhelming aspect of Khufu's creation: its size.

IMMORTAL STATISTICS

Let us begin with the bare figures. The Pyramid rose to 481 feet (146.6 metres) – the top 31 feet (9.45 metres), including the capstone, are now missing. According to early calculations, its base length was an average of 756 feet (230.42 metres). It contained approximately 2,300,000 separate blocks of stone, each weighing an average of 2½ tons. Some were much larger than this: the limestone casing blocks which once covered its exterior weighed 10 tons or more, and there are granite blocks in its interior known to weigh up to 40 tons. Its total weight was thus almost 6 million tons: more precisely, some 5,955,555 tons.

But, as anyone who has visited the Giza site will verify, these statistics do not really convey the sheer impact of the building, which is why so many writers are driven to comparisons and superlatives – pointing out, for example, that until the building of the Eiffel Tower in Paris in 1889, the Great Pyramid reigned supreme as the tallest building in the world; or that, at 6 million tons, it weighed more than all the buildings in the modern City of London's square mile put together. One much-repeated formula is that you could easily fit the Houses of Parliament and St Paul's Cathedral into its base area and still have room to spare. Another proposes that the cathedrals of Florence, Milan and St Peter's in Rome would all fit comfortably inside.

Those who prefer a more planetary scale might like to know that, if the Pyramid were sliced up into regular 12-inch (30 cm) cubes, and those cubes then placed in a row, they would stretch two-thirds of the way around the earth. It was Napoleon, no less, who appears to have initiated this particular

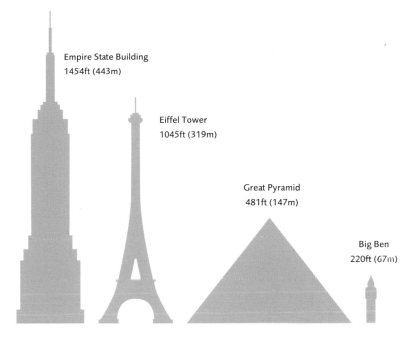

Empire State Building
1454ft (443m)

Eiffel Tower
1045ft (319m)

Great Pyramid
481ft (147m)

Big Ben
220ft (67m)

computational game. When his armies invaded Egypt in 1798, trailing groups of scientists and scholars in their wake and thus giving birth to the modern discipline of Egyptology, Napoleon declined the invitation to make a personal ascent of the Pyramid and instead occupied himself with pen and paper. On the return of his tired and sweaty underlings, he announced that if the three pyramids on the Giza plateau were dismantled, they might be used to build a defensive wall, 10 feet (3 metres) high and 1 foot (30 cm) thick, along the entire perimeter of France. It would appear that Napoleon's skills as an amateur mathematician rivalled his flair as a general, for one of his scientists rapidly corroborated these figures. (Or perhaps that sage, a Monsieur Monge, was merely an accomplished flatterer.)

The Great Pyramid was the tallest building in the world until the completion of the Eiffel Tower in Paris in 1889. This diagram shows its size relative to that structure, plus two other world-famous landmarks.

Once these brain-confounding figures have been digested, one can pass to the next most astonishing aspect of the Great Pyramid. It was not only the largest that Egypt had ever seen, but the most accurately constructed. The base of the Pyramid is level to within less than an inch (2.1 cm). The average deviation of the sides from their alignment to north, south, east and west is a tiny fraction of a single degree: 3 minutes 6 seconds. The four corners of the Pyramid are almost perfect right-angles. Its angle of slope is a remarkably exact 51 degrees 50 minutes 40 seconds. It used to be estimated that the sides of the Pyramid were identical to within less than 8 inches (20 cm), with dimensions of: north 755.43 feet (230.26 metres); south 756.08 feet (230.45 metres); east 755.88 feet (230.39 metres); and west 755.57 feet (230.3 metres). More recent calculations, however, suggest that it was even more accurate than this – accurate, in fact, to within less than 2 inches (4.4 cm). And this is not even to mention some of the most truly remarkable feats of planning and engineering which may be found in the Pyramid's complex and wonderful interior, especially its Grand Gallery and King's Burial Chamber; a whole recondite world which requires a lengthy account in its own right.

When a structure of such overwhelming dimensions has been executed with such astonishing precision, it is easier to forgive those who wish to attribute its

making to supernatural forces. But, as this book will try to explain, no such leap into the unknown is required. For all its daunting magnificence, the Pyramid is the work of human beings; and before we proceed to examine its secrets in more detail, we need to encounter one human being in particular – the man known to the Greeks as Cheops, to the Egyptians by the formal name of *Khnum-khuf* ('the god Khnum is his protector') and to present-day scholars by the abbreviated form of that name: Khufu.

KHUFU

This ruler came to the throne of Egypt in about 2551 BC, inheriting it from his father Sneferu, who may well have reigned as long as half a century. Although there are still disputes and uncertainties about exact datings, the history of ancient Egypt is conventionally divided by modern historians into thirty or thirty-one Dynasties, beginning around 3100 BC and ending in 332 BC. Sneferu was the first king of the IVth Dynasty (2575–2465 BC) and Khufu the second. Historians have also arranged the various dynasties into nine main periods; the second of these is known as the Old Kingdom, runs from 2686 to 2181 BC and is made up of the IIIrd, IVth, Vth and VIth Dynasties.

The Old Kingdom was the golden age of pyramid building, which is why it is sometimes referred to as the Pyramid Age. As we shall soon see in greater detail, the earliest forms of pyramid, known as step pyramids, started to be erected in the IIIrd Dynasty under a king called Djoser (2630–2611 BC). True pyramids did not emerge until the reign of Sneferu, which means that Khufu's builders were working with an extremely novel form of architecture: one calculation has it that barely sixty years elapsed between the completion of Djoser's pyramid and the beginning of Khufu's, which means that someone who was a child in Djoser's reign could, with luck and good health, have watched the first stones being put in place at Giza. Khufu's own monument – the largest and most extraordinary that Egypt would ever see – was soon joined by the smaller but none the less gigantic pyramid built near his own at Giza by his son Khafre (also known as Chephren: 2520–2494 BC), and then by one considerably smaller still, although in any other surroundings it would seem highly imposing, built by his grandson Menkaure (also known as Mycerinus: 2490–2472 BC).

Menkaure's pyramid was the last flourish of the art for the IVth Dynasty, and although the Vth and VIth Dynasty rulers also built a number of pyramids,

Opposite
This tiny ivory figurine, just 3 inches (7.6 cm) high, is the only image of Khufu that is confirmed by inscription. Seated, dressed in a kilt and holding a flail, the body was found without its head by the British Egyptologist Flinders Petrie in Abydos in 1903. Realizing the significance of the king's Horus-name (*above*), inscribed on the front of the throne, Petrie stopped all other excavation at the site. After three weeks' intensive sieving of sand and minute examination of the surrounding area, the head, wearing the crown of Upper Egypt, was found.

they were on a much more modest scale. After this, in the time known as the First Intermediate Period, pyramid building virtually ceased, and was not revived until the Middle Kingdom (2040–1640 BC), and then only fitfully.

In all, about ninety pyramids have survived to the present day in one form or another, although some of them are little more than rubble-strewn sites, their original forms unidentifiable save to the trained eye. Almost all the products of the Pyramid Age were built just to the west of the Nile, on the edge of the desert, in a thin strip running from Meidum in the south to Abu Roash in the north – all, that is, within easy reach of the ancient capital and home of the royal palace, Memphis.

In the context of the long sweep of Egyptian history, therefore, pyramid building was an art which developed swiftly, peaked early and went into almost immediate decline. The vast pyramids which have haunted the imagination of the world were built in the course of just three generations: the reigns of Sneferu, Khufu and Khafre. Add all the eighty-five-odd pyramids of all the rest of Egypt together, and they still only amount to 41 per cent of the total mass of stone used by those three monarchs.

In terms of sheer bulk, Sneferu must be judged the greatest of the pyramid builders, since it has been estimated that his pyramids alone – disregarding the complexes in which they stood – contained some 124 million cubic feet (3.5 million cubic metres) of stone. But for individual size, grandeur and technical perfection, the laurels must go to Khufu. The Egyptians called the Great Pyramid *Akhet Khufu* – 'The Horizon of Khufu'.

Sadly, little is known of Khufu himself. It is a small irony of history that the only known image of the man who commanded the building of the Great Pyramid is a minute figurine, no more than 3 inches (7.6 cm) high, found at Abydos; it is marked with his Horus-name, *Her-Mejedu*. It is fairly certain that he was quite young when he came to the throne; the inference is that he wished to compete with, and outdo, the amazing achievements of his father; the impression is given that he may have been overweeningly arrogant – but then, as Pharaoh, he was in effect a god.

Still, even if relatively little is known about the man, a very great deal is now known about his creation; and to explore it is one of the most enthralling of all journeys in imaginative history. To stand at the start of this journey is to be in much the same position as that of Howard Carter when he peered into the newly opened depths of Tutankhamun's tomb on 26 November 1922.

'Do you see anything?' his companion, Lord Carnarvon, asked nervously.

'Yes,' Carter replied. 'Wonderful things.'

CHAPTER ONE

THE PYRAMID
AND ITS SITE

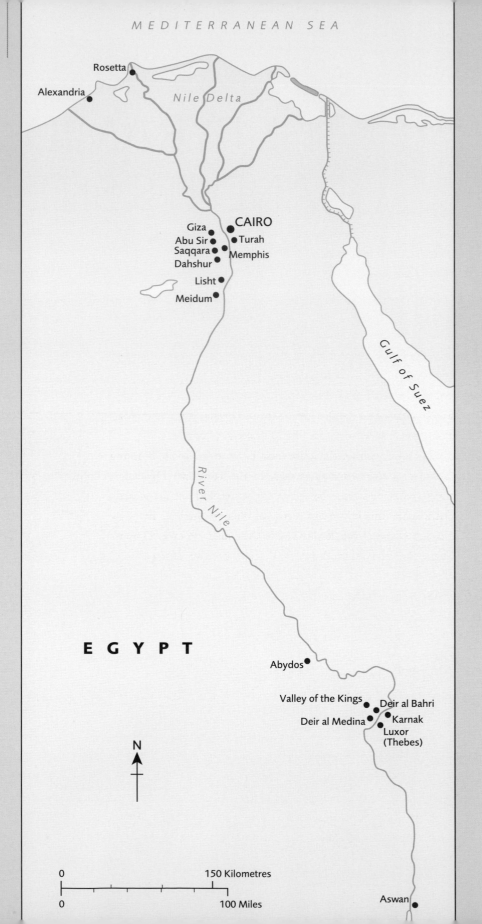

MEDITERRANEAN SEA

Rosetta

Alexandria

Nile Delta

CAIRO

Giza

Abu Sir ● Turah

Saqqara ● Memphis

Dahshur

Lisht

Meidum

Gulf of Suez

River Nile

E G Y P T

Abydos

Valley of the Kings ● Deir al Bahri

Deir al Medina ● Karnak

Luxor
(Thebes)

N

0   150 Kilometres

0   100 Miles

Aswan

BEFORE THE BUILDING STARTED |

DJOSER, IMHOTEP AND THE STEP PYRAMID

IN THE COURSE OF HIS REIGN (2575–2551 BC), Khufu's father Sneferu – the first king of the IVth Dynasty – constructed four of the greatest buildings Egypt had ever seen. Most famously, he built the two colossal tombs at Dahshur, known respectively as the Bent Pyramid and the North Pyramid, as well as the smaller one at Seila. According to most modern accounts, Sneferu was also responsible for much, if not all, of the similarly remarkable pyramid at Meidum. These four monuments were, in fact, the earliest manifestations of what is now understood by archaeologists as the true pyramid form, and marked a major advance on the existing monumental structures, the IIIrd Dynasty step pyramids.

Before Sneferu's time, the history of royal tomb building had fallen into two main stages. In the first two Dynasties, kings and nobles were buried in fairly simple brick structures. Then, some time in the nineteen-year reign of the IIIrd Dynasty Pharaoh Djoser, from 2630 to 2611 BC, the man who was Djoser's Chancellor and High Priest of the sun-god Ra designed and built the first step pyramid on a site in Saqqara, overlooking Memphis. His name was Imhotep.

Later generations of Egyptians regarded Imhotep as a sublimely gifted astronomer, a magician and the father of medicine; eventually he was deified, and regarded as the son of Ptah, the principal god of Memphis. When the Greeks conquered Egypt in the third century BC, they identified Imhotep with their own legendary founder of the healing arts, Asklepios. Imhotep has thus come down in myth and folklore as the mysterious, divinely inspired 'inventor' of the pyramid: not altogether true, but not wholly without foundation, either.

Imhotep's design provided the earliest model from which all subsequent pyramid complexes, including Khufu's, were developed. What he built was a huge enclosure, covering some 37 acres (0.1 of a square kilometre, the size of a substantial town at the time) and protected by a limestone wall 34 feet (10.4 metres) high and 5397 feet (1645 metres) long. Within the walls were many

Page 17
Computer-generated aerial view of the Great Pyramid nearing completion.

Djoser, the IIIrd Dynasty pharaoh for whom the first step pyramid was built. Once painted, and with eyes inlaid with crystals, this life-size limestone statue was found in 1925 in a *serdab* on the north side of the king's step pyramid at Saqqara.

buildings, some functional, some dummy – pavilions to the north and south, terraces, façades, columns, chapels, statues and more. Towering over all of these was his greatest feat: a prototype pyramid, rising in six large steps to a height of about 197 feet (60 metres), with a base of 397 by 358 feet (121 by 109 metres) and containing 11,668,000 cubic feet (330,200 cubic metres) of clay and stone. Excavations have shown that this was built in several stages, and started with a square *mastaba* – a simple raised tomb structure.

And like its illustrious descendants at Giza, Imhotep's pyramid was no mere pile of rocks. Below ground level, its builders carved out 3½ miles (5.6 km) of huge shafts, tunnels, vaults, galleries, stairwells and passages – an underground complex on an unprecedented scale. Part of this complex, presumably intended to be a subterranean palace for the king, is beautifully decorated with blue faience tiles evoking the waters of the Egyptian Netherworld, and with raised limestone bands simulating the appearance of a reed mat.

Djoser's resting place was a vault of granite blocks, sealed off after his burial with another granite block weighing 3½ tons. Three of the panels in the underground 'palace' show Djoser performing a ritual, and his *ka* statue (which represented his 'soul' or 'spirit') was placed in a *serdab* (chamber) built in alignment with these apartments. Explorations of Djoser's step pyramid have turned up evidence of other burial sites, including two intact sarcophagi as well as some forty thousand plates, cups and other vessels, mainly Djoser's inheritance from his ancestors. The site has other splendours and mysteries, but its true significance for our story is that Imhotep's genius initiated the particular forms of tomb building which culminated in the Pyramid of Khufu.

SNEFERU AND THE BIRTH OF THE TRUE PYRAMID

When Sneferu inherited the throne of Egypt, Djoser's tomb was the only complete, large-scale pyramid in the land. He decided to follow Djoser's example, and ultimately followed it four times over: in terms of sheer scale, at least, he deserves to be known as the greatest of all the Egyptian pyramid builders. In the light of recent research, it appears that he began at Meidum by staying fairly close to Imhotep's basic design and constructing another step pyramid – the centrepiece, again, of a major necropolis. Later, though, he appears to have changed his mind and sent workers back to Meidum to fill in the original steps and remould his monument into a true pyramid, of the smooth-surfaced kind we recognize

Designed and built for Pharaoh Djoser by his Chancellor, Imhotep, the step pyramid at Saqqara initiated a form of royal tomb building that would culminate in the Great Pyramid at Giza.

today, with an exterior slope of 51 degrees 50 minutes 35 seconds: in other words, very nearly the same as Khufu's Pyramid. When completed, this structure was 302 feet (92 metres) high and had a base length of about 473 feet (144 metres). The Egyptians came to call it 'Sneferu Endures'.

The history of this later development is clouded by the ruined state of the Meidum structure. Today, it consists largely of a three-stepped tower surrounded by a mound of debris. Did the whole thing start to collapse while still under construction, as some have conjectured? This now seems unlikely, since no bodies, ropes or timbers from the IVth Dynasty have ever been found in the rubble. Or was the work suddenly abandoned on the very eve of completion, perhaps because of Sneferu's unexpected death and the accession to the throne of an aggressive young man with plans of his own? The simplest, and probably best, guess as to what happened is that the pyramid was indeed completed, that looters subsequently stripped away its outer limestone casing, and that generations of later builders set about using it as a handy quarry. Certainly, the archaeologist Flinders Petrie reported that it was still being used by local builders as a free-for-all quarry at the time of his excavations in the early 1880s.

In addition to smoothing out the sides so that they rose to a summit, Sneferu's other main innovation was in the pyramid's internal structure. Workers built a long descending passage (very much like that in the Great Pyramid), with an entrance at about 54 feet (16.5 metres) above the base and running down, by way of a short horizontal passage and a vertical shaft, to a central corbelled burial chamber – quite

Sneferu's Southern Shining Pyramid, or 'Bent Pyramid', at Dahshur.

small, just 19 feet (5.8 metres) long and 9 feet (2.7 metres) wide – roughly at the level of the original desert surface. Adapted in various ways, this interior arrangement became a standard pyramid feature, as did some other innovations.

Meanwhile, in the long interval between the building of the step pyramid at Meidum and its later adaptation, Sneferu had commanded two other monuments. Round about the fifteenth year of his reign, he shifted operations some 25 miles (40 km) north of Meidum to Dahshur, where he set about building another necropolis. The twin crowns of this project were two great pyramids.

One of them, known to the Egyptians as the Southern Shining Pyramid, is referred to today by a more straightforwardly descriptive title: the Bent Pyramid. It rose from the sands at the sharp angle of 54 degrees 27 minutes 44 seconds, but then, about halfway up, continued at the much gentler slope of 43 degrees 22 minutes to the summit. Why the abrupt change of angle? Probably because the builders were faced with subsidence problems: there is evidence that the Bent Pyramid was originally designed as a much smaller structure with sharply rising sides, at about 60 degrees or so. When this proved dangerously unstable, they added a stone 'girdle' around the base – the 55 degree side. The gentler slope of the upper section can be accounted for by an urgent change in the method of laying stones: the method so far used, with the stones sloping inward, turned out to increase the stresses on the pyramid and reduce its stability. The final part of the building was made with the stones set horizontally.

Sneferu's other full-scale pyramid at Dahshur was the North or Red Pyramid, known to the Egyptians as the Shining Pyramid. Some time around the thirtieth year of his reign, and perhaps prompted by the imperfection of the Bent Pyramid, the king suddenly gave up work on the southern structure – although, as at Meidum, he later went back and had it completed – and shifted his attention to making a new, rather more elegant tomb with sides set at the much gentler angle of 43 degrees 22 minutes. Its height was to be 345 feet (105 metres), and its base length 722 feet (220 metres).

The pyramid's interior developed the lessons of Meidum and its older sibling, the Bent Pyramid. Again, workers made a long descending passage, running from an entrance high up on the north side down to ground level, where it joins two almost identical antechambers, both corbelled and with high roofs. A short horizontal passage leads from the second of these to the main burial chamber, 50 feet (15 metres) high and also designed with a corbelled roof. The largest of the secondary structures in the vicinity of the North Pyramid is a mortuary temple, now mostly destroyed, perhaps finished in a hurry, and planned on a modest

The Shining Pyramid, also known as the North or Red Pyramid, at Dahshur.

scale. It seems likely that Sneferu was actually entombed here, rather than in the burial chambers of any of his pyramids. If so, his death was attended by a melancholy irony: the greatest of all pyramid makers did not, after a lifetime of prodigious effort, manage even a short post-mortem tenancy of any of his magnificent tombs.

And so Sneferu's third son and immediate successor, Prince Khufu (2551–2528 BC), came to the throne, blessed with the inheritance of an all but perfected pyramid form, yet burdened with the challenge of outdoing his father's achievements by building something still more imposing. How would he do it?

KHUFU'S SEARCH: LOCATION, LOCATION, LOCATION

History knows the scale of Khufu's solution, but before work could begin on his staggeringly ambitious monument, Khufu had to determine a suitable site. Every possible location would have to fulfil at least five basic requirements. For religious reasons, it would have to be built west of the Nile, in the region of the setting sun. For safety reasons, it would have to be located higher than the Nile's flood plain. For logistical reasons, since many of the building materials would be transported by river, it would have to be as near as safely possible to the Nile's bank. For political and social reasons, it would have to be reasonably close to the Egyptian capital, Memphis, and perhaps also to one of the king's smaller palaces. Finally, for geological and architectural reasons, it would have to be based on solid bedrock with no obvious cracks or weaknesses, and in a plain which would be suitable for the construction of level foundations.

There were several plausible candidates, all of which would eventually be the home to Old Kingdom pyramids. Saqqara – site of Imhotep's step pyramid for Djoser, and long a burial ground for Egypt's elite classes – was always a tempting possibility for the pharaohs: it would eventually provide a base for no fewer than eleven royal pyramids, more than any other location in Egypt, and hundreds of other minor pyramids, *mastabas* and tombs. It is fair to regard it as a full-scale City of the Dead, since it was well over 4 miles (6.4 km) long at its fullest development. Both Saqqara and Abu Sir were in easy sight of Memphis, Saqqara being a kind of other-worldly twin to the living capital. Other possible building sites included Sneferu's old choice, Dahshur, some 5 miles (8 km) to the south of Memphis; Abu Roash, 17 miles (27 km) to the north; and Meidum, 33 miles (53 km) to the south. In the end, Khufu opted for a site just a few miles downriver from Abu Roash, on the northwestern corner of the Giza plateau, at the edge of the desert and about 5 miles (8 km) from Giza itself.

Here lies a gigantic plate of limestone known to modern geologists as the Mokkatam Formation, about 1310 yards (1200 metres) across on a diagonal from SSE to NNW, and rising to a height of 197 feet (60 metres). The southeast corner of Khufu's Pyramid, and the southeast corners of the two smaller pyramids built on the same site over the next two generations after his death by Khafre and Menkaure, are aligned on the so-called 'great Giza diagonal' which runs at roughly 43 degrees east of true north. Together, these three pyramids comprise the single most famous and instantly recognizable piece of architecture of all time.

THE PROBLEMS OF LEVELLING AND ALIGNMENT

THE FOUNDATION CEREMONY

FOR A MOMENT, let us jump forward a little in time to the day on which Khufu performed the foundation ceremony for his life's great work. There are very few written records detailing any aspect of pyramid design or construction, and most of those that have survived date from around a thousand years later. The fullest of these texts indicate that when a king inaugurated a pyramid, he would first observe the position of the stars in the Great Bear, and then, with the aid of a priest personifying Thoth, ibis-headed or baboon-shaped god of writing and measurement, he would mark out the base lines of the four outer walls.

However, thanks to a fragmentary relief from the Vth Dynasty, it is possible to arrive at a much closer and more vivid portrait of the ceremony conducted by Khufu – broadly similar to the later pattern, but with telling idiosyncrasies. It would have gone something like this. Dressed in state, Khufu proceeded to the Giza site accompanied by a priestess personifying the goddess Seshet, Thoth's feminine counterpart. Both Khufu and his priestess carried a golden mallet and a cord with a peg at the end. The priestess hammered her peg into the ground at a prearranged spot. Khufu then aligned his cord to the heavens, stretched it taut, and drove in the second peg, thus indicating the precise axis on which his temple was to be aligned. To be exact, he used the visor of the priestess's head-dress as a pointer in the direction of a particular star, known to the Egyptians as the 'hoof' star in the constellation of the Bull's Foreleg, and to modern astronomy as Benetnasch, part of the familiar constellation of Ursa Major, the Great Bear.

An impressive performance, no doubt. Yet, solemnly as the ceremony was carried out, it was more in the nature of an official seal of approval than a genuine act of calculation. Khufu was, of course, not really discovering an astral correspondence, but rather giving formal, regal notice that the calculations of others met with his favour. The actual process of alignment, far more complex and painstaking than this quick glance at a predetermined star, had been worked out carefully in advance by his *savants*.

Records show that one of the principal tools used in this alignment was an invention called a *merkhet* – literally, an 'instrument of knowing', or, more loosely, an 'indicator'. In later foundation ceremonies, the Thoth priest carried one as part of his ritual equipment. In its most basic form it consisted of a horizontal bar, a raised block and a plumb-line. It could be used either on its own or in conjunction with another instrument, the *bay* – a straight palm rib with a V-shaped slot cut in its wider end. In differing forms, it was used as a solar clock during the day (by noting the length of the shadow cast on the bar by the block) and as an astral clock at night (by noting the height of a given star above the horizon).

As already seen, the results that could be achieved by this simple device were impressively accurate; and the Great Pyramid is the most accurately aligned of all the pyramids of Egypt, with an average deviation from true north of little more than 3 minutes of a degree. The exact scales of accuracy are north 2 minutes 28 seconds south of west; south 1 minute 57 seconds south of west;

The *merkhet* was the principal piece of ritual equipment used by the Thoth priest during alignment ceremonies.

Reconstruction of the
alignment ceremony.

east 5 minutes 30 seconds west of north; and west 2 minutes 30 seconds west of north. Now recollect the equally impressive accuracy of the foundation – level to within less than an inch (2.1 cm). Of all the questions that have haunted amazed visitors to Giza over the centuries, few are as irresistible as this: how on earth was such stunning precision achieved?

Many scholars and scientists have laboured at these problems, and though no answer has been accepted in every last detail, at least some of the methods used by the Egyptians are now as clear as they have been for four millennia.

LEVELLING THE BASE

One much-repeated hypothesis of how the Pyramid's base came to be so close to perfectly flat involves the use of water. According to this theory, builders drew on Egypt's immemorial farming traditions, built shallow walls of Nile mud all around the construction zone and then poured in water until it reached an appropriate level. Workers would then cut a series of trenches beneath this shallow pool, making sure that the bottom of each trench was exactly the same distance beneath the water's surface. Then the water could be drained off, and the space between the trenches carefully carved out until the rock was perfectly smooth and level.

There is a pleasing simplicity to this theory, and it may be partly supported by the archaeological record – sure enough, there is a grid of trenches quite close to the north side of the second Giza pyramid, where work on levelling (if that is what it is) was given up before completion. But the water theory has met with a number of objections.

One or two are obvious: the Old Kingdom had no more efficient way of transporting water than in pots carried on poles, so that evaporation and drainage would surely have thwarted even the most large-scale attempt to build an artificial pond. It is hard, moreover, to work very precisely under water with hammers and chisels. A variation on the water theory suggests that, although grids of trenches were indeed dug, what the workers did was to mark the exact surface level, drain the water and then proceed with the levelling by following the marks. But there are problems with this proposal, too.

The strongest arguments against the water theory are geological and architectural. The architects who designed the Pyramid of Khufu, and later that of Khafre, were dealing with a sloping plateau that was originally 23–33 feet (7–10 metres) higher than the eventual base, and in both cases they left a massif of rock jutting up into the centre of the pyramids. They confined their cutting and filling to the task of levelling a strip around these massifs; and for Khufu's Pyramid they levelled not the bedrock but the pyramid's foundation platform.

The principal contesting theory takes its cue from the lines of holes, still visible on the Giza site, that run at roughly regular intervals parallel to the sides of the Great Pyramid (as well as Khafre's). Since their spacing is not exact enough to be of any real use as a measurement of length, the likely explanation is that they were used to hold stakes with a long cord strung along them, which could be used in conjunction with a *merkhet* or ordinary plumb-line to establish exact heights and then be conveniently removed when the builders needed to move in a new stone.

Using these guide lines, it is now thought, the builders were able to achieve exceptional precision by carefully adjusting the level of the Pyramid's foundation platform, not that of the raw bedrock on which it rested. The foundation platform was made of very high quality Turah limestone, occasionally backed up with local limestone. As the ascending courses of limestone were piled up, the central massif of bedrock was shaped by workers to fit each new course.

Khufu's priest holds up a pendulum to align the proposed pyramid site with the stars.

The process began with the builders stringing out a reference line extended to true north. Next came the job of laying out a square with precise right-angles. Now, since the large chunk of natural bedrock jutting out in the middle of this square would have prevented them from taking sightings of the square's diagonals, they must have used one or more of three basic methods of measurement. The first, which relies on the use of a set-square identical in all essential ways to our modern tool, is unlikely to have been the sole method, since it would have demanded a set-square much larger than any of those known to have existed in Egypt.

The two other, more plausible, methods are geometrical. One uses the so-called Pythagorean triangle – familiar to schoolchildren learning about the square on the hypotenuse being equal to the sum of the squares on the other two sides, and almost certainly known to the Egyptians of the Old Kingdom, who appear to have used this method in mortuary temple design. The other, a calculation based on the intersection of arcs, assumes that the builders might have mapped out overlapping circles using a cord as radius and a pole as central point of rotation. One easy answer to the vexed question of how the Egyptians could be so accurate in their building is that they were good at geometry.

ALIGNMENT WITH THE HEAVENS

The greater and more complex puzzle is that of the Pyramid's alignment with north. Two principal theories hold the field: the solar and the astral.

In its traditional form, the astral theory proposes that the Pyramid's builders would have erected a temporary wall, circular in shape, several feet in diameter and just tall enough to exclude the sight of everything but the night sky from the point of view of a person standing inside. In short, the wall was an artificial horizon – and, as that term implied, had to be perfectly horizontal along its top. (The water method, tricky if not impossible to accomplish on pyramid scale, might have been perfectly feasible for building a much smaller structure like this.)

All the Egyptian astronomer-geometer would then have to do was pick a given star in the night sky, mark its setting and rising points on the top of the wall, use a plumb-line to extend those marks to the bottom of the wall, and then join them at the centre of the circle. Bisect the resulting angle and, behold: true north!

The solar theory incorporates some rather cryptic references in later Egyptian texts to 'the stride of Ra', Ra being the sun-god. According to this theory, the Eyptians used not a wall but a pole stuck into the ground: more properly, a gnomon. The pole is stuck in the ground, as close to perfectly vertical as can be achieved with a plumb-line, and its shadow on the ground measured three hours before noon. That length is marked on the ground and used as the radius of a circle. As the sun rides higher in the sky the shadow grows shorter, and then, in the afternoon, lengthens again. At the point when the shadow once again touches the circle, it forms an angle with the direction of the first shadow. Once again, the bisection of that angle gives true north.

The exact application of these methods is uncertain: the wall-building astral method is in principle more accurate, but a great deal more troublesome, since it would seem to have required the building of circular wall after circular wall to ensure that the pyramid's base line did not start to deviate. A line of solar gnomons certainly seems a more convenient option, and modern attempts at reproducing an extended line north using solar calculations has proved fairly reliable.

It is possible, though, that neither of these widely discussed methods was the one used by Khufu's team. In 2000 Kate Spence, a scientist from Cambridge University, pointed out a very curious fact about the levels of accuracy in pyramid alignment. Up to the reign of Khufu, alignment became progressively more accurate; after the reign of Khufu, the accuracy began steadily to decline.

What had gone wrong? Had the geometers and astronomers simply become less painstaking? Had they somehow lost the refinements of technique that had been won over the previous generations? Or does the answer lie elsewhere?

Spence came up with an ingenious suggestion: to see how she arrived at it, we must examine the astronomical phenomenon of precession. The celestial North Pole is the point around which all the stars appear to be rotating. Now, since it is actually the earth which is turning on its axis, and not the stars which are spinning around the earth, it follows that this apparent central point is directly in line with the earth's axis of rotation. However, that axis itself is not perfectly stable, but itself rotates somewhat like a gyroscope, though at a rate imperceptible to the naked eye since its complete cycle takes some twenty-six thousand years.

Calculations show that there was no single star exactly aligned with north during the pyramid-building period of ancient Egypt. Kate Spence's suggestion is that Egyptian astronomers would, instead, have identified two other stars located on either side of the Pole. When these two stars are vertically aligned above the northern horizon – an alignment which could be checked with a *merkhet* or plumb-line – they give a precise reading for true north. She went to the records, and found that there are two sets of candidates which could have been used in just this way.

The first pair of stars would have given an accurate reading of north at around 2467 BC; the second would have been accurate at 2443 BC. The date of the first of these coincides fairly closely with the dates arrived at by archaeological methods, although, if this conjecture is correct, it means that the alignment would have taken place some seventy years later than has formerly been estimated. The details of the alignment debate are still a matter of dispute; no reputable scholar, however, disputes that the alignment was achieved by some form of celestial observation.

So much for the mysteries of geometry, astronomy and faith – the privileged knowledge of the king and his elite company of priests and nobles. It is time to meet the men who turned Khufu's ambitious vision into overwhelming reality with sweat and strain: the army of conscript builders.

CHAPTER TWO

A CONSCRIPT'S LIFE

MYTH AND REALITY

Previous page
Reconstruction of a typical village
scene in IVth Dynasty Egypt

EVERYONE KNOWS THAT THE PYRAMIDS WERE BUILT BY SLAVES. Everyone has seen or heard about those Hollywood-on-the-Nile epics with titles like *Land of the Pharaohs*, or the children's picture books on life and times in ancient lands, or the silly cartoons: cruel overseers cracking whips, burly slaves tugging or shoving giant rocks, emaciated slaves giving up their last dying breath under the pitiless desert sun. Some may even remember, or half-remember, that it was a classical historian – Herodotus, no less, the father of History himself – who explained that the human infrastructure on which the pyramids was built was slavery. And everyone is wrong.

It is now known that slaves played no part in the making of Khufu's Pyramid. In modern terms, his workforce was something much closer to a temporary army – an army whose 'soldiers' were healthy young men recruited from the towns or the farmlands. Nor was this recruitment for work on the Pyramid an unprecedented phenomenon: on the contrary, it was part of a much broader network of social obligations and ties.

A still from Howard Hawks's 1955 epic movie *Land of the Pharaohs*. Hollywood filmmakers, like everyone else, assumed that the pyramids had been built by slaves rather than by conscripted labourers.

Conscripted labour – some modern accounts call it 'corvée' labour, a kind of tax paid with work rather than goods – was the essential fuel of every major construction project. Roads, canals, mines, public monuments – all were built or dug by conscripts. The only difference between such projects and Khufu's was the dizzying scale of the Great Pyramid – that, and (we can reasonably guess) the sense of pride and purpose that must have eased the harshness of labour just a little. The practice of corvée labour was so firmly established in the Egyptian scheme of things that, as will be seen later, important people were buried with miniature figurines, intended to take on any corvée labour that might be demanded of the dead person by the gods.

Moreover, whether they went to their task willingly or otherwise, these were young men who, for all the undoubted dangers and difficulties of their new life, might well have enjoyed a far better and more rewarding life in the service of their king than they would had they stayed peacefully at home in some distant, impoverished village. They were regularly and (with some exceptions) well fed, housed in barracks, given superior medical treatment; and, however humbly, they were working for the king.

Archaeological work in recent years has yielded a good deal of evidence to support this radically revised view of the pharaoh's workforce. For example, one important tomb bears the inscription: 'His Majesty desires that no one should be compelled to the task, but that each should work to his own satisfaction.' No more than a pious sentiment? Surprisingly, perhaps, the instruction appears to be quite genuine, although this is no guarantee that overseers took any notice of it. Other documents help to confirm the hypothesis that young men must have come and carried out their construction service much as other young men have done their military service across the centuries – grumbling and reluctant, perhaps, and sometimes dodging it if they could, but still with a sense that they were facing their clear duty as male subjects. Some may well have believed that, in helping the king towards his immortality, they were also improving their own prospects in the next world.

In any case, for most workers the period of conscription was quite brief – sometimes as short as a single wet season; only a hard core of highly skilled workers and administrators stayed on the project for year after year. Conscripted men could often nominate a substitute, and it appears that a discreet payment to the local scribe might ensure that one's name was kept off the recruitment list.

The clearest way to explore and rediscover the reality of the pyramid builders is to look more closely at the kind of rural community from which much of the workforce was recruited, and the kind of life that young men bound for Khufu's project would have known up to the day on which the king's summons came.

LIFE ON THE FARMS

Using all the solid information which modern archaeology has put at our disposal it is possible to reconstruct the key elements of Egyptian country life some four and a half thousand years ago. The Nile, then as now, was Egypt's life-blood. The annual ebb and flow of its current was the central fact of life for all Egyptians, and the nation itself was really just a narrow ribbon of fertile land some 630 miles

The Nile, photographed by the *Landsat* satellite. The Nile Delta can been seen towards the top of the picture, with the Gulf of Suez to the right. Beyond the fertile banks of the river the landscape is barren desert.

(1000 km) long, hugging the rivers and menaced on both sides by the desert. At the time of the pyramids, only 3100 square miles or just over 8000 square kilometres of the Nile's fertile flood plain was under cultivation. (Only in 1960 did the Aswan dam increase this figure almost five-fold, to 15,000 square miles or 37,500 square kilometres.) 'Egypt', Herodotus pithily wrote, 'is the gift of the Nile', and the people implicitly paid respect to their river in the names they gave their seasons. In place of our four divisions of the year into spring, summer, autumn and winter, the ancient Egyptians divided their year into three parts.

Peret or 'emergence' was a period roughly corresponding to our winter, running from mid-November to mid-March, when the flood waters drained from the fields and farmers could begin to work on their land again.

Shemu or 'dryness' lasted from mid-March to mid-July. The Nile sank to its lowest level, the fields drained completely dry and the soil began to crack and turn to dust. The harvest had to be completed by the early part of this season.

Akhet or 'inundation' ran from mid-July to mid-November. At this, the hottest time of the year, rain fell on the high ground and the Nile overflowed with life-giving water. It was impossible to work in the fields at this time, so most of the farmers remained at home and occupied themselves with domestic tasks, including the repair of their main tools – the hoe, the plough, the sickle.

They had other divisions of time, in some cases quite similar to ours. The working 'week' lasted for nine days, with the tenth a day of rest: this unit was called the *decan*. The ancient Egyptians divided their year into thirty-six *decans*, giving 360 days, and then bulked out the remainder with five 'epagomenal' days, each devoted to a different god or goddess: Isis, Osiris, Horus, Nephthys and Seth. They had not, however, hit on the handy convention of a leap year, so their calendar lagged by about a month every century. They also divided their day into twenty-four hours, although the hour unit was variable according to the season; and they calculated – following the hint provided by their fingers – on a decimal system.

Egyptian New Year was signalled by the rising of the star Sirius in mid-July, at the turning point between *shemu*, the dryness, and *akhet*, the inundation, when the previously sluggish waters grew deeper and flowed more swiftly. To the Egyptian mind, the rising star and the rising waters were parts of the same cosmic movement and, despite their predictability, were a cause for rejoicing.

The basic annual routine could be followed only when the climate was merciful. If the longed-for flood waters proved to be too high and powerful, they would sweep away everything in their path, including livestock and farmers: the death toll could be frighteningly high. At the other extreme, if the waters were too low the earth would remain parched, crops would fail, and famine – to the point of mass death from starvation – would all too often be the grim result. There is evidence that the collapse of the Old Kingdom was in part the result of the despair and anarchy wrought by a succession of low Niles.

Even in a good year everyday life for the peasant farmer was not easy. One of the few writers from ancient Egypt known to us by name, a scribe of the Middle Kingdom period called Khety, summed up the peasant's lot in some memorable phrases of his 'Satire of the Trades', and although he may have been exaggerating a little – he was trying to encourage his own son to learn how to write and so escape the wretched fate of farm labour – his words have the ring of unpleasant truth: 'The peasant groans unceasingly. His sound is harsh, like the cawing of a raven. His fingers and his arms run with pus and stink atrociously.

Fishing on the Nile. From a relief in the tomb of Princess Idut at Saqqara, *c.* 2410 BC.

He is weary of standing in the mud all day, clothed in rags and tatters ... and when he comes home in the evening, he is utterly exhausted by the walk.'

Almost everyone who lived in the village, except the priests, scribes and other officials, toiled on the land but did not own it. Devout people believed that only the gods owned the land, but the immediate reality was that the king owned the land, and that all the people who laboured on it were tied to the state, a temple, a tomb endowment or a royal cult. All peasants were registered, and, as we have just seen, if there was a shortage of labour in one area they may well have been moved summarily to another – for ancient Egypt was what we would recognize as a centralized nation state, the first of its kind in the history of the world.

Top Calving. Detail from a relief in the tomb of the vizier Kagemni at Saqqara, *c.* 2400 BC.

Above Butchers quartering an ox. From a relief in the tomb of Princess Idut at Saqqara, *c.* 2410 BC.

Although the peasants' work was undeniably hard, the soil of the Nile flood plain was highly fertile, and a smallish area of two *arouras* (one *aroura* being about 47 square yards or 40 square metres) could provide a whole year's sustenance for a single person. At *peret*, the start of the working year, the farmers began to plough the fields with the help of their wives and children. Ploughs were pulled by oxen guided by a ploughman, and the sower – often a woman – walked beside or behind, scattering grain from a basket into the furrow; children ran around scaring away the hungry birds. Then oxen were led along the same path, trampling the earth flat and pushing seeds well down into the soil.

The main crops were flax, emmer, wheat, barley, broad (fava) beans and chick peas. Flax was one of the most important of these crops, since it was used to make clothes for the living, shrouds for the dead, and ropes and nets for hunting and fishing; the oil extracted from its seeds was used as medicine. The toilers moistened the soil from buckets of water, slung from both ends of a pole carried across the shoulders – painful, back-breaking work. But they also used canals, blocked off as the Nile subsided each year so as to retain the precious water for a few weeks more.

Harvest time was also hard work, but it could be made a lot more bearable by the rituals that often accompanied it. Sometimes musicians would play and the villagers would sing as they attacked their crops with wooden or copper sickles:

Beautiful is the dawn of day that appears over the land;
a fresh breeze stirs from the north;
the sky obeys our desires;
come, let us work with a will!

A more material form of comfort was the cool beer they gulped while plying their sickles. Sometimes, too, the men made their work into a competitive sport, racing each other to reach the end of their furrows first, bragging and jeering when they won: 'Me, I'm a bloke who works fast! Who works even when he's talking? Me! Who's got a tanned chest and horny hands? Me! You, you're bone idle!' The agricultural scenes painted on the walls of *mastabas* were often decorated with words like this, and with other snatches of typical field conversation, bragging, warnings and banter: 'Go on, steer it properly. Hurry up there with those oxen! And look lively, the master is there and he can see what you're doing!' ... 'I'll do even more than the master wants!' ... 'Hurry up and finish your work so we can get home early!'

When the sheaves had been cut, the women and children gathered them in nets and loaded them on to donkeys, which carried them off to the threshing floor just outside the village. The same donkeys – sometimes joined by oxen – then threshed the grain by walking around in circles on top of it. Then women, wearing shawls over their heads to protect them from the dust, winnowed the grain – separated out the impurities – and let the wind blow away the chaff. Finally, the harvested grain was taken to the local granaries under the supervision of scribes, who then set about assessing how much tax the village had to pay the central state.

This annual routine of ploughing, sowing and harvesting of crops was the basic work of life, but higher officials and other members of the ruling elite also supervised and reaped the pleasures of more luxurious kinds of cultivation. Take the example of Metjen, a well-known high official of these IVth Dynasty days, who enjoyed a domain of 200 cubits (about 340 feet or 103 metres) long and the same wide. His garden, enclosed within walls, was richly planted with beautiful trees, including trees which yielded ripe figs and other luscious fruits, and grapevines, from which copious quantities of wine were made.

All such gardens had their vines, harvested during the inundation months of August and September when work in the fields became impossible. And besides the figs and grapes, these gardens also provided dates, pomegranates, cucumbers, melons, peas, cabbage, horseradish, parsley and lettuce, as well as many spices, including anise, cumin and coriander. Nor were the pleasures of the eye and nose neglected: Egyptians loved flowers – cornflowers, poppies, chrysanthemums, irises, hyacinths, mandragoras, larkspur, water lilies and jasmine – cultivating them whenever possible and using them in their homes or as ritual offerings.

The village also kept animals, both for food and for labour. Apart from the oxen and the donkeys at work in the fields, they kept herds of goats, sheep and pigs. Ducks, geese and pigeons were kept domestically; wild birds, like cranes, were trapped in nets. Dogs were valued as workers, but also as companions, and were given affectionate names; the rich sometimes had their favourite dogs buried in grand style.

Outside the village, cows were also kept by the nomadic herdsmen who spent most of their time in the marshes and swampland; less regulated than the

peasants, they none the less had to submit to a cattle count for their district every two years. After the count, the cattle were divided into two groups: those allowed to return to pasture, and those sent off to the slaughterhouse, to be killed and carved up under the watchful eye of the priest, who made sure that the ritual proprieties were observed. First the front hoofs were severed; then the rear hoofs; and then the heart and other vitals were removed.

This, then, was the basic working life of the rural world from which the men who laboured for Khufu's dream were gathered; changeless, in its principal features, over the better part of three thousand years.

HOME LIFE IN THE VILLAGE

The male children of the village would have lived within a fairly narrow range of experience, from birth to ritual circumcision at puberty. Birth was always a risky business for both mother and child. Women went into labour at home, kneeling or crouching over a platform made of two bricks set widely apart. A midwife – a professional wise woman – attended the labour and cut the umbilical cord, although only after the baby had been washed and the placenta expelled. The mother was then taken to a birth tent, where she rested and was purified, for it was believed that giving birth defiled a woman, and she must not return to the family home for a while. (It was also believed that conception could take place via the mouth.)

These were not the only beliefs and rituals mothers needed to know about. The high rate of infant and child mortality – as many as three or four out of five children would not survive to adulthood – was attributed to curses or evil

Geese. From a frieze in the *mastaba* of Princess Itet at Meidum, *c.* 2630 BC.

spirits. Mothers would pray to invoke the aid of the fertility goddess Taweret and of the protective deity Bes, the enemy of demons. Babies were named after a god, or after the pharaoh, or for some fortunate quality of their birth. They were nursed until the age of about three – rich women employed wet-nurses – and sometimes fed from clay baby bottles: dishes with long spouts. Raising children was the main work of women, and children were highly valued, not only in their own right but as a guarantee of descendants who would maintain the family's funeral cult. Families who were both healthy and fortunate may have had anything from ten to fifteen children.

Servant girls carrying fowl, livestock and, on their heads, baskets of bread and fruit. From the tomb of Ti, a senior official, at Saqqara, c. 2450 BC.

Women married as soon as they were physically mature: at about twelve to fourteen, so as to ensure the maximum number of fertile years. Men were allowed or expected to marry when they were slightly older, and had proved that they were good enough workers to support a family of their own. At fifteen, boys were already regarded as adults: if they were very lucky indeed, they would reach old age and be grandfathers, but most people, men and women alike, could expect to die by the age of thirty.

Marriage was a social rather than a religious or legal institution – in fact, there was no word in Egyptian to express the concept of 'marriage', although words and titles equivalent to 'wife' and 'Mrs' did exist – and in essence amounted to an agreement to live together and raise children. There was little in the way of a formal ceremony – just a celebration by the village, followed by the bride moving into her husband's house. Polygamy, although not banned, was rare, but those men who could afford it may well have taken a concubine or two and had children by them. Concubines had a much lower status than wives. Unfaithful wives, on the other hand, met with brutal punishments, including execution followed by the burning of the corpse and the scattering of its ashes on the Nile – the most terrible of all punishments, since it destroyed the means of future existence. Divorce was permissible if the wife proved sterile or unfaithful, but in practice was quite rare.

Sexual *mores* were, predictably, different higher up the social scale. Royalty and high officials took a number of secondary wives, and the pharaoh had a harem – important less as a source of erotic pleasures in the kingly bedchamber than for reasons of diplomacy, since the recruitment of these women generally helped to consolidate a long and complex chain of alliances with families throughout the land.

Wine was not the preserve of the rich alone: all Egyptians were fond of wine, and no fewer than six kinds were available in the Old Kingdom. Wealthier Egyptians favoured the vineyards of the Delta and Faiyum areas. When times were good, Egyptians liked to eat fairly well, and fairly often. They had three meals a day: a substantial one in the morning and evening, and a light snack at midday.

The heart of every meal was bread and beer – the products, that is, of barley and wheat. As many as nineteen types of bread were baked in Egypt, and it was usually served spread with a purée of fava beans or other pulses. The beer was usually dark – light beers were for special occasions, such as festivals – and for those who preferred it, or were too young for alcohol, there was milk from cows, goats, ewes and donkeys. For the fortunate, this basic diet was supplemented by some of the protein-rich sources already noted: fish from the teeming Nile, meat from domestic animals as well as desert game – antelope, gazelle, ibex – sometimes in the form of a stew. Even the poorest people could afford to eat poultry occasionally, as pigeons, cranes, ducks and geese were there for the taking by clever hunters, and hunting was a favoured occupation of rest days.

Foods were mainly cooked in animal fats. Dishes could be flavoured with herbs or – an option only for the rich, for this substance was rare – sweetened with honey. Sesame, flax and castor oils were also available. Besides beans, the main vegetable in a peasant farmer's diet was the onion. Meals were eaten sitting on a rush mat, with food on a clay platter in the middle: stoneware was not used for everyday meals, but reserved for tombs. People used their fingers to eat, having washed their hands before the meal.

Beer brewers. Painted wooden model from a Middle Kingdom tomb, c. 2000 BC.

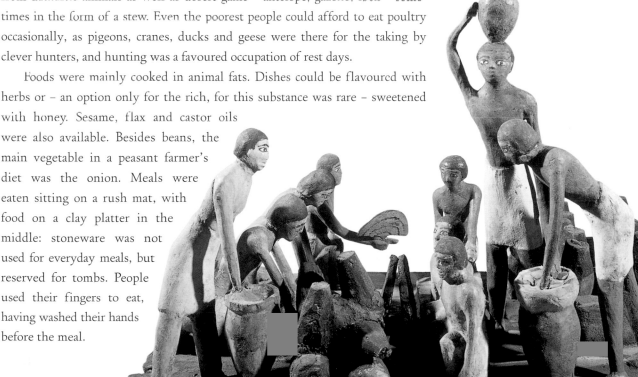

Village streets were narrow – often so narrow that, with arms outstretched, you could easily touch both sides. Houses were huddled closely together and the only openings to let in light and air were their front doors; pieces of coarse fabric were hung across them to keep out at least some of the dust. The Egyptians built their great tombs to last for eternity, but their houses were far more modest and far less durable. They were made mainly of sun-dried mud bricks, wooden beams and pressed clay – organic materials that disintegrated easily over the years. (Richer families did use some stone, especially for door sills and lintels.) Nor were they very comfortable, especially since they swarmed with pests: fleas in the coats of domestic animals; mosquitoes buzzing in the night air; worst of all, because it endangered the family's diet, rats and mice running free in the store rooms, for Egyptians had not yet learned to domesticate that highly useful sanitary tool, the cat, and would not do so for another thousand years, until the beginning of the New Kingdom.

There were other threats to health. Rubbish was either hauled off to the nearest canal, taken to a dump just outside the village, buried in holes left over from digging up building materials, or simply thrown outside the door to fester in the streets. There was no running water – the household supply, kept in pots, was fetched from the canal or river by the women, who balanced large jars on their heads.

Despite the tedium of this daily water-fetching chore, all but the roughest families were quite fastidious in their ways, carefully washing off the mud, dust and sweat of the fields at the end of every day with water poured from a jug, and taking full body baths from time to time in a small bath tub. Nobles took greater care still of their personal hygiene, and grooming played a large part in their daily lives. About a century after the building of the Great Pyramid, Ptahotep, the Pharaoh's Vizier and minister of justice (*c.* 2400 BC), is recorded as requiring no fewer than six servants for his levee: they clothed him, shaved him, arranged his hair, polished his nails and washed his feet. When ordinary folk wanted a shave they had to go to the local barber, who scraped them with a stone blade as they squatted at his feet.

Even some of the humble houses had a lavatory of sorts, in the form of an earth closet. Richer houses had a structure made of stone blocks with a half-full bucket of sand in between; sometimes, these structures even had a lid. In the words of Herodotus, from *c.* 500 BC: 'The women pass water standing and the men sitting. They go indoors to ease themselves, but they eat their food in the open, saying that indecent needs should be met in private, but decent ones in public.'

The floors were made of pressed clay or brick paving tiles. In fine houses and palaces, the floors would have been polished to extreme smoothness, and then painted over with stucco. Mats – made from reed, papyrus and palm leaves – were laid over the top to make them cool to the feet even in the hottest weather, and so that dust would fall through the gaps in the fabric and not be constantly kicked up.

Furniture was sparse: usually just a built-in bench in the living room and sometimes a low table for eating, with a few seats in the form of low stools, as well as low platforms for sleeping. Mats cushioned the hardness a little, and head-rests did something to ease the pain of tired necks. Wall niches and the occasional wooden chest provided storage for the household linen and plates. All the household clothes were made by the women – a difficult task, since the basic tools were thick needles of bone or bronze, hard to manipulate. If they had time to make more clothing than their own family needed, they were allowed to

A kitchen scene depicting men and women preparing bread and beer from barley and emmer wheat. Painted wooden model from the tomb of the nobleman Meketre at Deir al Bahri, c. 2000 BC.

club together with similarly industrious friends and sell the extra garments in a shop, under the control of a Directress of Weavers.

Clothes were simple, hardly changing at all in basic design throughout the Old Kingdom, and, with a few major exceptions, were a good deal less important as a badge of social rank than is usual in most stratified societies. Men generally went bare-chested, and wore a short loincloth – a single rectangle of material tied at the waist and falling to just above the knee. Some officials wore a long starched skirt which covered most of the body and was held up by a cord around the neck; some priests wore a leopard-skin slung over one shoulder.

For women, the basic garment was a long dress which fitted quite tightly to the body, emphasizing slenderness, and was held up by two shoulder straps: judging by its representation on statuettes, it would not look much out of place in a fashion magazine today. Court ladies occasionally adopted a long-sleeved tunic with a V-neck, elaborately decorated with sewn motifs. Almost everyone went barefoot; the habit of wearing sandals would not become commonplace for a good five hundred years or more.

Egyptian women, like this offering-bearer, typically wore closely-fitting long dresses with shoulder straps. Painted wooden model from the tomb of the nobleman Meketre at Deir al Bahri, *c.* 2000 BC.

But the simplicity of basic dress did not mean that the Egyptians set no store by the arts of personal adornment. On the contrary, a surprising part of the non-working day was given over to various forms of grooming by all but the very poorest. The dressing of hair was carefully attended to, and those who showed unusual flair for the task could often improve their station in life by going to work for a great household. The value placed on a gifted barber was well indicated by the traditional story of the hairdresser to the pharaoh who accidentally dropped a ritual object during a major ceremony and yet – almost unbelievably – was pardoned.

Men and women alike shaped their hair – or their ceremonial wigs, used for religious festivals – with combs made from wood and bone, and kept it in place with beeswax or resin. Vanity was as commonplace here as in most other societies: there were endless potions for dyeing hair, stemming hair loss and otherwise fighting the advancing signs of age. And both sexes indulged freely in the use of make-up, especially eye-liner, which was made from kohl, derived from galena (lead ore) found in the mountains near the Red Sea shore. It was held not only to beautify the face, but also to guard the eyes against the constant threat of infection from blown dust and dirt. Hair, hands, feet and nails were all tinted red with henna; fragrant oils were used to soften the skin and make the body smell sweet.

Jewellery played a still larger part in everyday life, not only as adornment but as an instrument of magic. Children ran around with good luck amulets on bracelets, pendants or rings: each of these bore a single hieroglyph meaning 'life', 'health', 'endurance', 'prosperity' and the like. Rings in the shape of scarabs were sometimes inscribed on the flat side with a spell or the name of a god, thus providing daily protection from demons. One major fashion of the Old Kingdom was the *usekh* collar, made of several rows of cylindrical beads in blue and green faience. The higher up the social scale, the more lavish and conspicuous was the jewellery. Princes and princesses wore pectoral adornments of precious metal; Khufu's mother, Hetepheres, filled one of her tomb-offering chests with twenty bracelets of ivory and silver.

At the centre of every Egyptian house was the fire, tended by the women. This burned either in the open-roofed kitchen, or in a courtyard. Mothers cooked over a fireplace, bricked in on three sides, or on a small, portable clay oven: a sort of pan, equipped with a conical stem for hot charcoals. There was often a small bread oven, and a 'saddle quern' – used to grind grain into flour. Besides charcoal, the principal fuels were animal manure – cow dung was a particular favourite – vegetable waste and scraps of timber. Fires were started by the heat from friction – a fire drill of hard wood, spun back and forth in a piece of softer wood. It was usually best to cook outside if possible, since ventilation was poor and people could inhale a dangerous amount of smoke.

At night, light from the fire was augmented by small, oil-burning lamps. There was not a great deal to do in the dark hours by way of amusement, but equally there was no very strong sense that looking for pleasure once the day's work or the season's work is done was in any way sinful or shameful. As Ptahotep writes, tolerantly:

> Do not shorten the time devoted to pleasure ...
> Do not lose time in daily work, once you have
>   done what is necessary ...
> When your fortune is made, follow your desire,
> For a fortune has no savour if one is gloomy.

Most households possessed small percussion instruments, used partly to accompany dancing but also in the fields, to encourage workers at their tasks, as well as to frighten away evil spirits and protect the dead. Some also had flutes and reed instruments, with three to four holes in their stems. Music, song and dance were everyday pastimes, and came to the fore at times of feasting.

For the aristocracy, the range of leisure pursuits was far wider. At banquets, dancing girls performed a kind of ballet, young men fought each other – sometimes to the point of serious injury – and music was played on more elaborate instruments, including the harp, famous as an instrument of love. A song popular at such banquets, the words of which are inscribed on many private tombs, reminded listeners of death but only to encourage them to feel all the more keenly the pleasures of life:

This limestone statue of Nofret, the wife of Prince Rahotep, depicts the princess wearing eye-liner and an *usekh* collar. Meidum, *c.* 2610 BC.

> *No one has ever come back from below*
> *to tell us their state,*
> *to tell us their needs,*
> *to comfort our hearts ...*

Rejoice, then, while you are alive! ...
Follow your heart and your happiness ...
For lamentations save no one from the pit!

Egypt was a profoundly hierarchical society, and might, indeed, best be represented in diagram form as a pyramid. The broad base of the pyramid was composed of the peasant farmers. Above them were the artisans – the skilled craftsmen. Then there were what might be called the professional classes – the priests and scribes. Scribes, who attributed the origin of their fiercely protected mystery to the god Thoth, possessed the rare qualification of being able both to read and to write. (Probably less than 5 per cent of the total population was so much as passably literate.) This was a skill which was handed down from father to son, and thus allowed those families so privileged to live comfortable lives for many generations, spared the miseries of manual labour. They were, so to speak, the nervous system of Egyptian society, gathering, transmitting and storing all the basic information of its social and economic life. Without writing, there could be no central state.

Women singing and playing the harp. Relief on the false door of Nikaure, c. 2420 BC.

Priests had bureaucratic as well as ceremonial functions to perform, and were not necessarily all that well versed in knowledge of the gods. One of their most important functions was the cleansing and care of the cult statue in the local temple – a task which, strictly speaking, was the prerogative of the king, but which for obvious practical reasons was delegated to chief priests throughout the kingdom. The profession was not too demanding, being organized on a shift basis – the Egyptians called such a shift a *saw* or 'watch' – so that the average priest only worked in the temple for one month in every four. Priests were required to wash themselves ritually four times a day, to be shaven clean of all body hair and to abstain from sex during their period of office. A number of priestesses – women of high birth – were dedicated to the goddess Hathor.

A variety of local overseers and other kinds of secular official, most of them from the upper classes, and substantial landholders in their own right, all

deferred to the most important secular authority in the region, the governor (or what historians call a 'nomarch', after the Greek word for the regional divisions of Egypt, 'nomes'). But he, too, had a relatively low place in a hierarchy which ran all the way up to the royal court in Memphis, and ultimately to the Vizier – in effect, the pharaoh's 'prime minister', in charge of every function of the state: agriculture, taxes, justice and construction. Above him, and above all mortals, was the pharaoh: supreme priest, supreme landowner, supreme judge, supreme warrior, supreme being.

Young men fighting. Detail from a frieze in the tomb of the royal manicurists, Niankhkhnum and Khnumhotep, at Saqqara, c. 2450 BC.

THE CALL-UP AND THE NILE JOURNEY TO GIZA

It was to the rural communities that the king's men came to recruit young men for royal service. The village mayor, the nomarch and their attendants would have gathered in the middle of the village. The attendants shouted out the names of those who were to be conscripted and the conscripts would then have been taken to the edge of the village where their hair was shaved to the bare scalp. Then, having said goodbye to their families and with their clothes packed in a bundle, the young men would have been led across the flood plain to the banks of the Nile, where a large transport boat was waiting to take them to Giza. Although the parting would have been sorrowful, it is reasonable to suppose that their sorrow was mixed with a sense of pride: they were, after all, doing their manly duty to the king.

For village boys recruited in the south, the journey to Giza was of almost unimaginable dimensions: 500 miles (800 km) or more – a distance which would

Reconstruction of a barge carrying conscripts from the villages up the Nile to Giza.

have taken at least a week, even in high summer when the Nile, which flows from south to north, streamed high and fast. Those travelling up the country from Aswan would have passed by almost all the great places of Egypt. To the east, Luxor (later known to the Greeks as Thebes) and Karnak. To the west, sacred Abydos and smaller urban settlements. Further north, the signs of civilized life and grand building would have become ever more frequent, especially to the west. They would have passed several of the sites we have already encountered in our survey of pyramid history: Sneferu's Meidum, then Dahshur, then Saqqara, then Abu Sir; and, off to the east, the great capital city of Memphis, home to the pharaoh himself. And as they sailed on, their boat would have pulled over from time to time to take on yet another small band of conscripts, conspicuously young and with newly shaven heads.

Once the barge had arrived at Giza, the conscripts, clutching their bundles, would have been marched up to the plateau. At length they would have seen a wall of mud brick, standing no less than 30 feet (9 metres) high, at the heart of which stood a towering gateway, known to historians as the Gate of the Crow. Beyond this gate was the workers' city of the Giza plateau: their new home and new workplace. The moment of passing through the Gate of the Crow was of great significance for the conscripts. Once they had crossed its threshold they were no longer villagers. They were Egyptians in the service of Khufu, living incarnation of the god Horus.

CHAPTER THREE

BUILDING THE GREAT PYRAMID

MATERIALS: THE KHUFU QUARRY

Previous page
Labourers using an A-frame
and ropes to haul stone blocks up
into the King's Burial Chamber.
(Reconstruction)

THE MAN CHARGED WITH OVERSEEING THE CONSTRUCTION of the Great Pyramid was Khufu's younger brother, Hemiunu – about whom, sadly, very little else is known. We have already seen some of the reasons why Khufu and Hemiunu might have chosen Giza as a suitable site: its relative flatness; the religious significance of its location to the west of the Nile, in the realm of the dead ruled by Anubis; its proximity to the nation's capital, Memphis; and so on. But there was one other crucial factor not yet mentioned. This largest of all pyramids, like every other pyramid, would have to be built close to a plentiful – in fact, practically inexhaustible – source of the right types of stone. And for this reason, perhaps above all others, Giza was ideal.

Today, visitors can see the evidence of its aptness in the formidable shape of what is now called the Khufu Quarry – a vast chunk in the approximate curve of a horseshoe that has been gouged out of the plateau about 1000 feet (300 metres) south of the Pyramid itself. At its deepest point, the quarry floor is very nearly 100 feet (30 metres) below its original surface level. Modern calculations have established that roughly 97.5 million cubic feet (about 2.76 million cubic metres) were cut from this quarry – although not all of it went to Khufu's Pyramid: despite the modern name, the other constructions on the Giza plateau also drew on this source.

Curiously, even an archaeologist as brilliant as Flinders Petrie was unaware of the exact presence of this giant excavation – although he knew, of course,

Remains of the limestone
casing on the eastern side
of the Great Pyramid.

that such a source must have existed somewhere in the vicinity – because it had long since been filled with millions of tons of clay, sand, gypsum and limestone scraps. It was only in the 1920s and 1930s, the better part of half a century after Petrie's pioneering excavations, that all of this geological rubbish began to be cleared away, revealing the full extent of the Khufu Quarry.

On its high, sheer, west face, masons of a later date than Khufu's reign have carved tombs, including three for the children of his son Khafre – a good sign that active quarrying must have stopped there at some time in the generation immediately after Khufu's death. Many other stones were brought to the Giza site in the course of construction, notably the fine white limestone used for its casing, brought in on barges from quarries to the east of the Nile: those at Mokkatam, Maasara and, above all, Turah. Still, it would not be far wrong to say that it was the Khufu Quarry which gave the Great Pyramid its main body. The question which inevitably leaps to mind now is one that science has only been able to answer with any real accuracy in very recent years: how many men did it take to build the Great Pyramid?

Many stones were brought to the Giza site on barges from quarries to the east of the Nile.

LABOUR: THE WORKFORCE

The task that faced our conscript workers was on a daunting scale. As we have seen, the Great Pyramid consists of about 2.3 million blocks. Each block is, on average, about 35 cubic feet (1 cubic metre) in size and weighs about 2½ tons. According to a document known as the Turin Papyrus, it is quite possible that the whole structure was built in just twenty-three years or less. The not always trustworthy Herodotus tells us that the labour took twenty years. Other

Overleaf
Reconstruction of
the Khufu Quarry.

sources imply that thirty years, or even slightly more, is also a well-founded possibility. Work was only done in daylight hours, which gives a ten-hour working day. If the terms of labour at Giza were similar to those elsewhere in Egypt, the men would have been allowed one day in every ten to rest and recover. A rough calculation based on these figures suggests that something like thirty-four stones would have been laid in place every hour: that is, slightly more than one block every two minutes.

On the face of it, this would seem to require a workforce of vast, almost unimaginable size: Herodotus, again, said that the Pyramid was built by one hundred thousand men, although there is some dispute as to how precisely that claim should be understood (see page 113). But the surprising reality is – as has been shown by a combination of recovered documents, excavations and the experimental re-enactment of stone-cutting and stone-moving by a modern team – that the actual number of people working on the Pyramid at any one time was far, far smaller than has generally been believed.

To see why this is so, we have to think in terms of what economists have taught us to call the division of labour. At its most basic level, the task of building a pyramid has three distinct stages: cutting the stones; moving the stones to the building site; setting the stones in place. Let us examine them one by one.

CUTTING THE STONES

Using the Turin Papyrus figure of twenty-three years as the total time for completion (and remembering that it may have been some seven years longer, in which case the daily workload was a good deal lighter than we are assuming), we can calculate that workers would need to have quarried just over 11,000 cubic feet (a little more than 300 cubic metres) of stone every day. The most reliable information on the manpower needed for such a task comes from an experiment conducted by the American archaeologist and leading authority on the pyramids, Dr Mark Lehner of Harvard University. Dr Lehner's experiments showed beyond reasonable doubt that a dozen modern-day workers, barefoot and with only an iron-cabled winch to give them any technological advantage over their counterparts of forty-five centuries ago, could readily shift between eight and nine stones of average size every working day.

So, to compensate for this machine-age advantage, Lehner 'allowed' his hypothetical ancient working team another twenty men – a total of thirty-two

per team. This means that the number of men required to move that sum of 11,371 cubic feet (322 cubic metres) each working day is 1212 – a fair number, to be sure, but not unimaginably vast.

Conscripts hauling a block of stone up a quarry ramp.

MOVING THE STONES

Using some of the same basic figures, we can start to estimate the number of haulers required. The average block weighs about 2½ tons. The slope up from the quarry to the building site is about 6 degrees, and runs for about 1000 feet (just over 300 metres) to the nearest side of the Pyramid.

Archaeologists have known for some time that when hauling blocks the Egyptians used what has whimsically been called a kind of 'railway' system – a set of parallel wooden staves, set down into the ground in the manner of railway sleepers, and coated with alluvial mud. If the mud is kept wet – by busy teams of water-carriers, running backwards and forwards, slopping the contents of large jars across the sleepers – these tracks make for admirably smooth hauling, and it is possible for quite a small team to manhandle very large blocks across them. One such 'railway' has been found at another pyramid site, Lisht, not far from Giza. Research at Giza has yet to turn up the remains of any such 'railway', but the procedure was sufficiently well known that it is safe to assume the presence of such tracks from the quarry to the Pyramid.

Various efficiency tests of this Egyptian 'railway' system have been carried out. One of the earliest, at Karnak, found that it was possible for three men to pull a 1-ton block down such a lubricated track – hence the approximate calculation that one man can be expected to move about 1/3 ton (about 340 kg) on his own. More recently, trials have shown that a dozen men can easily pull a 2-ton stone, even up a slight gradient, provided that it is also mounted on a wooden sled of the kind that Egyptian art records.

Now, the basic sums. If one man can move 1/3 ton (340 kg), then it takes just eight (in fact, seven and a half) men to move the average pyramid block of 2 1/2 tons. Assuming that it takes about an hour to make the 2000-foot (610-metre) round trip from the quarry to the building site, then one team could make ten trips a day. It would therefore take thirty-four teams to complete the amount of moving required: 340 stones a day. (Remember that these are averages, and that some of the stones are much bigger while others are considerably smaller.) So as not to exaggerate the strength and efficiency of each team, let us introduce a generous margin of compensation and assume that it was actually made up of, say, twenty men rather than eight, and that on average they were only working half as quickly as the modern teams – who, after all, only had to do the job for a few days, not twenty years. Even making such generous allowances, the whole job could easily be done with 1360 haulers.

Running total for the workforce so far: 1360 plus 1212 equals 2572 men. We are still well within the realm of the imaginable. Now for the final part of the construction process.

SETTING THE STONES

Here, considerations of the number of men who can usefully put hand to stone must come into play. Modern trials have shown that stones can be manoeuvred and set most efficiently with a team of six to eight men: up to four using levers, two to supply brute strength and make adjustments, and two trained stone-masons to do the trimming. Allow two more men for good measure, and the basic setting team is ten men. Estimate, as we have done above, that the haulers are delivering stone at the rate of thirty-four blocks an hour. If the stone-setters could keep up with this – and if they could not, some terrible production bottlenecks must have occurred – we arrive at the figure of 34 blocks times 10 men equals 340 setters. Apply the usual liberality, and grant that the process may only have been half as efficient as its modern counterpart, then as many as 680 setters may have been required.

Add it all up: 1360 cutters, 1212 haulers, 680 setters – and you find that, with twenty years to complete the task, it is quite possible to build the apparently superhuman structure of the Great Pyramid with a total workforce of not more than 3252 people, perhaps fewer, working at any one period. Again, it is not a tiny figure, but certainly within our realm of comprehension.

At this point, we can bolster the authority of all our basic arithmetic with knowledge derived from written sources. These suggest to us that the largest single unit of the pyramid workforce was a crew numbering around two thousand men, divided into two gangs of a thousand, both of which were then subdivided into five groups, each two hundred strong, known in Egyptian as *zaa* – a term later translated into Greek as *phyle*: 'tribe'. Graffiti from a later pyramid – Menkaure's – includes a beguiling human detail: one of the thousand-strong gangs called itself 'Friends of Menkaure', while the rival gang called itself 'Drunkards of Menkaure'.

Lifting a stone block on to the second layer.

Each of the five *phyles* had a more formal name: the 'Great' (or 'Starboard'), the 'Asiatic' (or 'Port'), the 'Green' (or 'Prow'), the 'Little' (or 'Stern') and the 'Last' (or 'Good'). Finally, each of the five *phyles* was itself made up of smaller teams, usually ten containing twenty men each. If we need 3252 pairs of hands, then two of these two thousand-strong crews will do the job nicely.

Four thousand men: you could call it a small army. But, as anyone who knows about real armies will recall, it takes a lot of back-up workers to keep a single soldier in the front line: sometimes twice as many non-combatants as combatants, sometimes (especially in the full-scale wars of the twentieth century) many, many more.

THE BACK-UP WORKERS

To keep all those four thousand men cutting and hauling and setting stones, there had to be – among others – carpenters to make the 'railways' and sleds, water carriers to keep them slick, potters to make those water vessels (and others), toolmakers to keep up a steady supply of replacements and repairs, overseers to make sure the work was done efficiently, and scribes – many, many scribes – to keep a steady tally of what was being done and where. And, of course, an army marches on its stomach. There would need to be a corps of cooks and bakers and butchers and brewers; additional builders to construct the ovens in which they cooked, as well as the barracks in which the basic workforce was quartered. Digs undertaken since about 1990 onwards have found the remains of exactly these quarters, including canteen ovens so large that you can almost step into them. Scattered in and around them are piles of fish bones, barley seeds, emmer seeds and the moulds that grow on bread, all preserved in the sand. The quantities of bones from butchered sheep, cows and goats that have been dug up at Giza of late are enormous, although it is possible that their sacrifice may have been for purposes of religion, not nutrition.

Excavations have also unearthed a previously unknown cemetery, mainly of extremely small, humble tombs for the lowliest working men (although a few slightly grander constructions also exist, preserving the 'middle class', as it were, of the pyramid workforce – overseers, officials and sculptors who wanted their resting places to be like miniature versions of a pharaoh's tomb). When physical anthropologists examined these remains, they discovered not only the evidence of hard manual labour that one would expect – compressed lumbar vertebrae and the like – but also signs that almost everyone working at the pyramid site, men and women alike, suffered from arthritis. Although there is as yet no written evidence to suggest that women were ever set to doing heavy manual work, all this recent evidence points to the fact that they could be employed at activities much more strenuous and damaging than household chores.

The most common injuries, among skilled and unskilled workers alike, were fractures of the radius and ulna in the arm and of the fibula in the leg. Most of these appear to have healed fairly well. In some cases, however, it is clear that workers were killed by violent blows to the skull, which suggests alarming possibilities. Murderously harsh treatment of the idle or insubordinate? Fatal grudges and vendettas carried over from work into leisure hours? Gang riots?

Still, however hard and dangerous the work could be, there is also abundant evidence that the labourers received the best medical care available at the time; and that this was in many ways reasonably effective. The medical profession was highly stratified, with six major ranks from 'Ordinary Doctor' (*sinw*) up to the 'Overseer of Doctors from Upper and Lower Egypt', and was probably divided into specialized fields like those of our own time. Among other useful knowledge, Egyptian doctors recognized the importance of keeping wounds free from infection, and tried to do so by bathing them in a mixture of crushed peas, fir oil and ibex fat. Bleeding was controlled with plugs of vegetable fibre; and whether or not they guessed at the exact mechanism of blood circulation, they certainly counted pulses to determine

Top Conscripts on their way to the pyramid site.

Above Water-carriers kept the mud beneath the stone blocks wet to ease their passage from the quarry to the pyramid site.

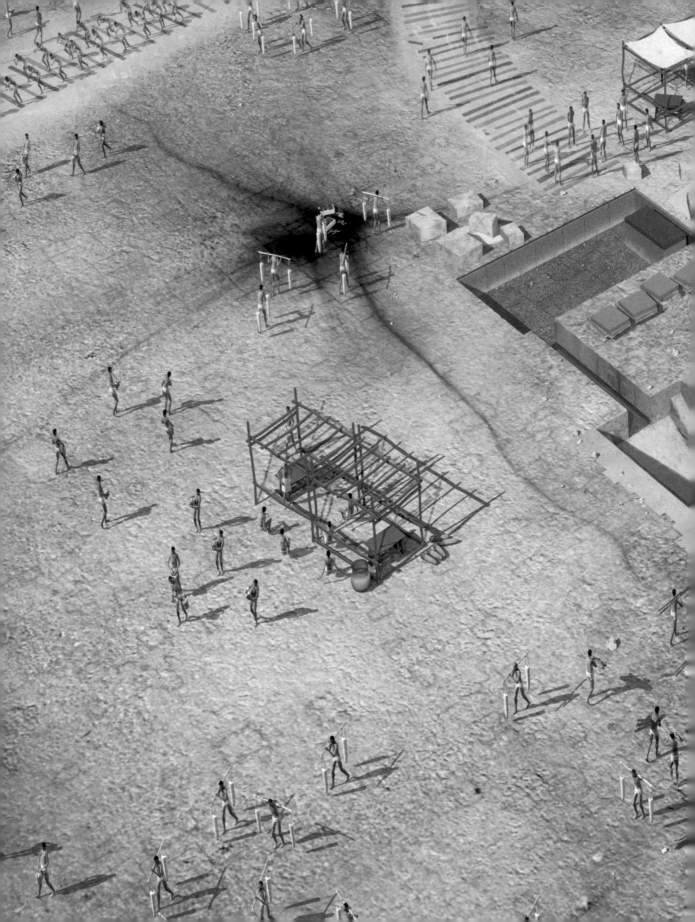

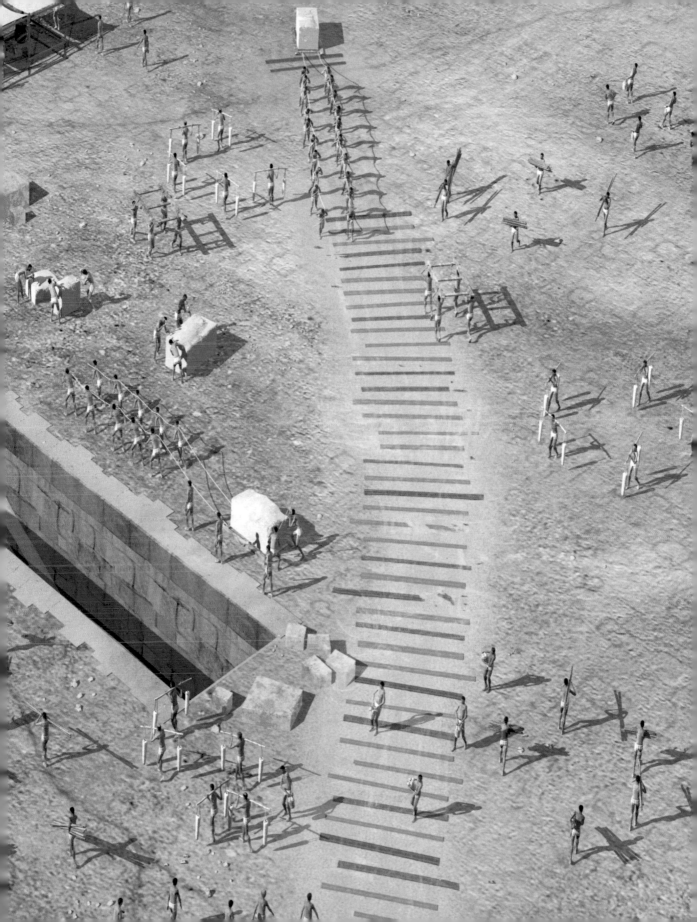

how the heart was beating. Splints were being used by the Vth Dynasty, and possibly a great deal earlier, and at Giza there are skeletal remains which confirm that the amputation of lower arms and legs successfully preserved the lives of several workers.

Oddly, despite the practice of removing perishable tissues for canopic vessels in mummification, the Egyptians were often hazy about the nature and disposition of inner organs. They seem to have had access to at least one drug, *ëspn*, known to soothe howling babies and possibly extracted from poppies. Since there was no intellectual distinction between empirical and magical knowledge, a good deal of 'alternative' medicine co-existed with the more practical kind, and the unskilled workers in particular seem to have preferred resorting to witch doctors of the kind they would have known from their home villages.

THE NATIONAL ECONOMY

Add all of these back-up workers together, and you arrive at a ratio of about five to one – that is, about twenty thousand or so secondary workers to four thousand primary workers, which gives something in the region of twenty-five thousand in all. During the years of building, the Giza plateau would have become a temporary town in its own right, noisy, dusty and ceaselessly in motion during the hours of daylight.

But that town is far from the whole of the story, as we know from many clues both small and large. For example, analysis of the fish bones found on site shows that many of these must have been imported, some from hundreds of miles down-river, since there is no other sign that these species ever lived in the waters near Giza. When a pyramid was being built, food and supplies poured into the site from all Egypt: not only fish but grain and loaves and cakes, oxen and pigs and geese, beer and wine – all of which would have to be variously tallied, stored, distributed, and, where appropriate, slaughtered. It took an entire nation to keep the workers cutting and hauling and setting. How did all these supplies reach the plateau? By means of Egypt's greatest blessing: the Nile.

Close to the site of the quarry Khufu's engineers built a large-scale harbour complex, linked by canals to the river itself. It was here that the barges and cargo ships, a common sight on Old Kingdom tomb reliefs, would pull in to unload their wares. The cargo ships, distinguished by the cabin at the stern, transported lighter materials: food supplies, but also small trees and scrub wood

This monumental, red granite head of a king wearing the white crown of Upper Egypt dates from the IVth Dynasty and is thought to depict Khufu.

to fuel the ovens of the bakers and cooks, and the forges of toolmakers. Heavier material mainly came on the barges: limestone, but also granite from Aswan, alabaster for pavements, gneiss for statues and other rocks for fine, detailed work. The stones could be extremely heavy: in the case of the red granite blocks for Khufu's Burial Chamber, as much as 40 tons each. They were mounted just above the barge decks using a set of strong wooden beams. When the barge pulled into dock, it appears, workers on the harbours would thrust levers between the stone and the deck, and so manoeuvre the blocks on to the shore where the hauling teams could take over.

To sum up: how many men did it take to build the Pyramid? As with many big questions, there are a number of good and justifiable answers, and the ones we can give today are better than most of those available to anyone since the Egyptians themselves. Unlike our forebears of the last couple of hundred years, who ventured all sorts of fanciful speculative responses, we can now confidently reply that, at any given time, it took roughly four thousand in the front line of construction, and twenty thousand by way of back-up crews. We do not know how often this workforce was replaced, but can assume that a central core of administrators, scribes, skilled craftsmen and others would have remained relatively stable, with replacements being made mainly among the two primary crews of two thousand.

But that reply, accurate as it is, leaves out all the resources that the Giza site drew to itself like a black hole sucking in light and matter. The fullest, truest answer to our simple question might well be that it took an entire nation to build the Great Pyramid.

METHODS OF BUILDING

Answering the beguiling question of 'how many?' has by now turned up a considerable amount of the equally tantalizing 'how?'. Given a fairly minimal technology of wood, slick mud and ropes, it is easily possible for a few barefoot men to move those great stones quickly and efficiently and in adequate quantities within the time available: no magic or extra-terrestrial assistance required (*pace* one very well-known book about meddlesome visitors from other planets which asserts, on no very clear grounds, that it would have been impossible for the Egyptians to build their pyramid in less than 664 years).

Equally, we have seen something of the geometrical, astronomical and architectural skills required to give the Pyramid its near-perfect alignment to the heavens and its beautifully exact dimensions. But this still leaves open the two questions of what the individual pyramid builder held in his hands, and how the work teams defied gravity to raise their stones so giddyingly high – 479 feet (146 metres) at the highest point.

TOOLS

We have already encountered some of the basic Egyptian tools of measurement: the plumb-line and bob, the gnomon (or pole) and the set-square; and we know that stones were shifted with ropes and wooden levers. Add to these a few fundamental extras – the hammer, the chisel, the knife, the drill, the saw – and the full arsenal of equipment available to the Pyramid builders is almost complete.

Limestone is not too hard to cut, and will yield readily to chisels and wedges: the Egyptians had been making high-quality copper tools, well suited to this task, since the Ist Dynasty – examples have been found at Saqqara. Examination of cuts at the limestone tunnel-quarries suggests that chisels were employed to slice blocks of limestone at the top and sides, and wedges used to detach it at the base; similar methods were followed at the surface, although the limestone of highest quality usually ran well below ground level.

Granite and basalt are far more resistant, and the question of how the Egyptians cut so precisely through these hard stones was long a matter of bafflement and dispute. Although fire and water may have helped to create superficial cracks in the stone to be quarried, it now seems that the most likely method was based on a painstaking process of abrasion. A copper saw or drill would be brought down on to a paste made of water, gypsum and quartz particles – quartz being the strongest component of granite. It was, then, the tiny quartz particles which cut into the rock, with the saw-blade or drill acting primarily as a means of ensuring accurate lines.

Investigations at the granite quarries of Aswan have also turned up hammer-shaped lumps of dolomite – a hard stone of a greenish colour, readily found in the eastern desert – weighing anything up to 15 lb (7 kg) which the digger would grasp in both hands and use to gouge out blocks, gradually turning these 'hammers' as the sharp edges became rounded down. (Discarded 'hammers', which had become completely rounded, could then be used as rollers for shifting heavy objects, such as sarcophagi.) The very fine-quality limestone used in the Pyramid's outer casing was shaped using extremely thin chisels, roughly $1/3$ inch (8 mm) wide. One last form of tool has also been

uncovered – pieces of stone shaped roughly like a large mushroom, with grooves worn into and across the head. These were presumably a sort of early, not very efficient approximation to a pulley. The true pulley does not seem to appear in Egypt until Roman times, two thousand years later.

The details of this small-scale construction technology are largely accepted. It is when one turns to the larger picture that debates begin.

Conscripts cutting stones in the Khufu Quarry.

RAMPS

Almost everyone agrees that raising the pyramid blocks above the first level must have required the use of a ramp, or several ramps. Those who dissent, and maintain that each level of stones was levered up course by course, have to confront the powerful arguments of Mark Lehner and other modern experimenters who have found that this method only really works for the uppermost levels, and not for the core or indeed the stones of the casing. They must also argue away the

Conscripts hauling a 50-ton block of stone up a ramp at the side of the Pyramid to the King's Burial Chamber.

unequivocal evidence that smaller pyramids of the IIIrd Dynasty were built with ramps, the remains of which have been uncovered by archaeologists. The only real question is: what sort of ramp or ramps; and, if more than one, how many?

The first point to consider is that all of these structures would have been huge, and one or two of them vast – temporary giants to rival the eternal giant they served during the twenty-odd years of construction. Where did all that material go when it was taken down? The answer, once the excavations of the 1920s were well under way, was as obvious as it was simple: the workers had followed the most immediately convenient method, and filled up Khufu's quarry with all the gypsum, tafla and limestone bits and pieces that had made up their ramp or ramps.

Let us examine the various candidates.

The Straight-on Ramp

This would have been built against just one side of the Pyramid. Advocates of this design are divided between those who maintain that it would virtually have covered an entire face, and those who hold that it would have covered only part of the face – meaning that it would be very tall, and also very thin at the top. To provide a slope suitable for the hauling teams, the incline could have been not much greater than one in ten, and the ramp would have had to be constantly lengthened as the Pyramid face sloped upwards and away – a tremendous drain on manpower.

The Spiral Ramp

This would have been a structure which hugged the outside of the Pyramid, spiralling inwards towards the summit. It could have been a single ramp, or it could have been a system of parallel ramps – as many as four, perhaps, one starting from each corner of the Pyramid's base. This would require much less material and manpower, but it would also mean that the unfinished outer case would have had to be similar to a step pyramid in order to accommodate the ramps. Evidence from pyramids of a slightly later date suggests that this solution was not adopted, although the signs are equivocal.

The Zig-zag Ramp

This is based on much the same principle as the spiral ramp, but is built on one side only.

The 'Envelope' Ramp

This is, in effect, a sort of all-over wrapping for the Pyramid, built up in much the same way that the outer surfaces of earlier step pyramids were built up, and then stripped away at the end of building.

The Multiple Ramp

This is simply a combination of two or more of the above.

The Internal Ramp
This is a ramp which runs right into the heart of the Pyramid, so that its masonry becomes part of the internal masonry as the structure rises.

At present, the best available evidence suggests that the most likely method would have been the multiple ramp: some form of spiral ramp, probably in combination with some kind of straight-on ramp, rising to about one-third of the Pyramid's eventual height and directed into one corner rather than into the centre of a side.

RAISING THE PYRAMID

As we know, Khufu's Pyramid was designed according to the very latest advances in Egyptian architecture – the modern expression would be state-of-the-art techniques. It was not until the time of his father, Sneferu, that builders abandoned the old technique of leaning layer after layer of stones at an angle. Sneferu's Bent Pyramid changed all that, substituting a system of carefully shaped horizontal layers at the edges of which were a row of blocks cut into the shape of trapezoids, so that their angled side created the exterior slope of the structure. Khufu's Pyramid followed the same pattern, and thus consisted of a central bedrock massif jutting up from the plateau (see page 27), surrounded and eventually covered first by layers of core masonry, and then by angled exterior masonry.

The laws of solid geometry tell us that the last stages of the Pyramid must have climbed up far more quickly than the lower ones: in a completely solid pyramid, 70 per cent of the total mass is concentrated in the lower third of the building, and no less than 80 per cent in its lower half. Only 4 per cent of the stones involved in the whole operation would have had to be raised above the two-thirds mark.

How did the designers manage to keep the angles so close to perfect and the dimensions so smooth as the structure rose? We know that this was no easy task, and seems to have grown harder the higher the structure rose – Khafre's Pyramid, for instance, exhibits a slight twisting effect towards the apex. (The quality of the core stone in Khufu's Pyramid becomes markedly finer as it nears the peak, almost as fine as the limestone casing, which suggests that the builders were aware of needing greater and greater control of their materials at such heights.) One indisputable technique that came into play as soon as the Pyramid rose above the level of the bedrock massif, and so allowed eyelines, was the sighting of diagonals across the Pyramid. Pyramids of a later date than Khufu's have also yielded evidence on their inner stones of vertical lines of red paint, marking the construction's central axis, and it is highly likely that the Great Pyramid would have been marked up with the same kind of guidelines.

The best available evidence points to the conclusion that the Pyramid face was designed stone by stone on the ground, with the masons checking and rechecking the fit of adjacent stones before allowing them to be hauled up and set into place. Each block was brought into position, checked, and then marked up with lines indicating the exact outer slope. At the end of the building process, as the ramps were gradually dismantled from the top downwards and began to recede, masons would fine-tune the process by using tiny chisels to chip away surplus stone until the faces were perfectly smooth. It is likely, although as yet not established, that the process of laying stones exactly would have been double-checked by taking eye measurements of the axes and diagonals, using purpose-built markers on the ground.

Manoeuvring the capstone into position.

Now, just one detail of the exterior remains.

THE CAPSTONE

At the top of every true pyramid is a *pyramidion* or capstone. That on the top of the Great Pyramid itself is long gone, but two of its close relatives survive to give us clues as to its appearance – one from a satellite pyramid of Khufu's own creation, the other from Sneferu's North Pyramid at Dahshur. Miniature pyramids in their own right, these capstones have been carved on the base so as to become convex, with four triangular surfaces. The upper surface of the matching stone was carved into an exactly matching concave shape: the capstone fitted securely like a peg in a hole.

Capstones from other periods have also been recovered. They are generally made of either limestone or granite, although there is a text in existence which implies that at least one capstone was coated with gold. One granite capstone, now in the Cairo Museum, is engraved with inscriptions appropriate to the various gods associated with the region towards which each of its faces was aligned: Harakhte in the east, and other deities including Anubis, Osiris and Ptah on the remaining sides. It is not known whether Khufu's capstone was similarly marked. Earlier suggestions that the outer surface of his Pyramid may have been painted in bright colours have now largely been discounted.

The process of setting the capstone in place was tricky and probably hazardous. The Pyramid was now far too tall to accommodate any ramps of the usual kind, so some archaeologists have conjectured the use of a series of temporary steps. Others suggest the use of some kind of scaffolding, since the Egyptians were known to use such temporary frameworks in their building, although it would have needed to be very strong scaffolding. In either case, a good clue to the emotions of the builders when the capstone was finally set in place is provided by a Vth Dynasty relief carving, which shows dancing, singing and other kinds of exuberant celebration.

But the celebrations would not have lasted too long. For one thing, there was an enormous amount of building work still to be done. With the ramp or ramps dismantled, the site was now open for the construction of all the other key elements of Khufu's necropolis – for, as in all the earlier pyramid complexes, the Great Pyramid is really nothing more (if nothing less) than the most spectacular feature of a whole complex of satellite pyramids, a mortuary temple, a giant stone causeway, a valley temple, a vast enclosure wall ....

And before we detail any of those creations, we need to stay with the Pyramid itself for a while longer. Thus far, we have only looked at Khufu's monument from the outside. The world inside those four vast sloping walls, now newly complete and gleaming white under the desert sun, is a good deal more remarkable in intricacy, ingenuity and symbolic portent than anything we have so far encountered.

CHAPTER FOUR

WORLDS WITHIN
AND WITHOUT

INSIDE THE PYRAMID: THE THREE CHAMBERS

PERHAPS THE MOST FASCINATING OF ALL THE ARCHITECTURAL TRIUMPHS of Khufu's Pyramid were reserved for its interior. It was Flinders Petrie who made the first exhaustive survey of these inner structures between 1880 and 1882, although earlier archaeologists had carried out surveys with a degree of accuracy which still commands respect from modern practitioners. Notable among these pioneers was Napoleon's employee Edmé-François Jomard at the turn of the nineteenth century, and the redoubtable British duo, Colonel Howard Vyse and John Shea Perring, who made their investigations in 1837–8.

The great modernist architect Le Corbusier famously defined a house as a machine for living in. Following his example, we could fairly speak of the Great Pyramid as a machine for the dead; or perhaps, more exactly, as a machine for resurrection. The inner structure is an ingenious machine indeed, made up of chambers, antechambers, open passages, hidden passages, shafts and portcullises. Fundamentally, though, it can be divided into three main areas, in ascending order: the Subterranean Chamber; the Queen's Chamber; and the Grand Gallery and the King's Burial Chamber. Why three chambers? Scholars are divided on the subject, some claiming that the basic plans changed as the building progressed, others that it represents a kind of emergency back-up system in the event of Khufu's unexpectedly early death, and others still that this three-part structure was planned from the outset.

THE SUBTERRANEAN CHAMBER

Before the Pyramid was sealed for eternity – as its makers vainly hoped – it could be entered by way of an opening on its north face, about 55 feet (17 metres) above ground level, and about 24 feet (7 metres) east of the central axis. From this point a descending passage, measuring about 3 feet 5 inches (1 metre) wide and 3 feet 11 inches (1.2 metres) high, cuts straight down through the masonry at an angle of 26 degrees 31 minutes 23 seconds. After 92 feet 6 inches (28.2 metres), it then hits the bedrock of the Giza plateau, but continues at exactly the same angle for another 99 feet 5 inches (30.3 metres), until it suddenly levels out and becomes horizontal for some 29 feet (8.8 metres) before

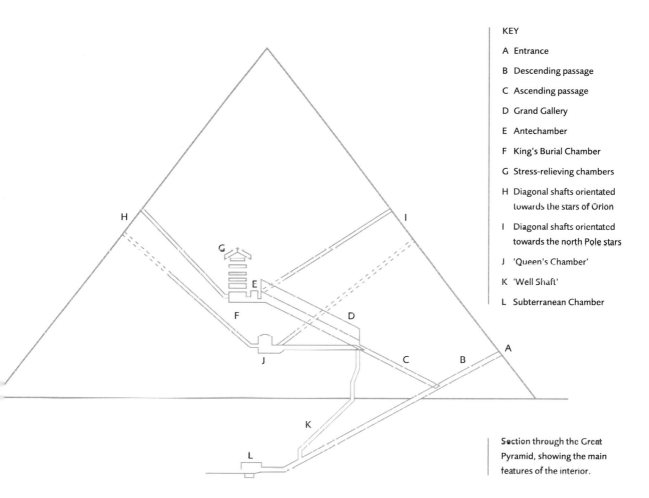

KEY

A Entrance

B Descending passage

C Ascending passage

D Grand Gallery

E Antechamber

F King's Burial Chamber

G Stress-relieving chambers

H Diagonal shafts orientated towards the stars of Orion

I Diagonal shafts orientated towards the north Pole stars

J 'Queen's Chamber'

K 'Well Shaft'

L Subterranean Chamber

Section through the Great Pyramid, showing the main features of the interior.

opening into a chamber 98 feet (30 metres) vertically below the plateau's surface. When Colonel Vyse and J. S. Perring first measured the chamber in 1838, they recorded that it was 11 feet 6 inches (3.5 metres) high, 46 feet (14 metres) from east to west and 27 feet 1 inch (8.3 metres) from north to south – accurate enough for most modern purposes, too, though a little misleading, since the chamber is unfinished. A square pit in the floor seems to have been the start of a scheme for making the chamber deeper, and the room's rough walls give the impression more of an abandoned building site than a completed design.

Thus far, incidentally, Khufu's Pyramid both follows the example of Sneferu's at Meidum (with a corridor descending to an inner chamber) and radically breaks with it (the corridor continues deep into the bedrock instead of stopping at ground level). There are puzzles here. From the southern corner of the subterranean chamber, opposite its entrance, a narrow passage barely wider

than a man's body extends horizontally into the bedrock. It looks very much as if this was carved by a single man (or, anyway, one man at a time), painstakingly cutting his way forward with a hammer and chisel. Was he making a sort of corridor to a projected matching second chamber? There was certainly a precedent for such a design, in the North Pyramid at Dahshur. Whatever the intention, this work was abandoned and no clue as to why has ever emerged.

Was this room ever really intended to be Khufu's resting place, as some excavators have guessed? If so, there is yet another mystery to tackle: the descending passage is simply not large enough to accommodate a sarcophagus. When the great Greek historian Herodotus came to Egypt in the fifth century BC, he was told by locals that beneath the Pyramid was a series of vaults built on a kind of subterranean island, enclosed by channels of water which ran below the Giza plateau from the nearby Nile. It was on this island, they said, that Cheops/Khufu was lying in state. (A sound historian in principle, if not always in practice, Herodotus carefully does not imply that he was able to verify these tales with his own eyes.)

Now, although this charming image has never been verified by so much as a scrap of material evidence, it does perhaps point to an enduring folk belief that the king had been buried beneath, rather than inside, his Pyramid. Was this just groundless rumour, or the muffled echo of an oral tradition reaching back two thousand years to the original phases of construction? Or, perhaps, of a handy lie propagated to put potential grave-robbers off the scent of the real burial place?

THE QUEEN'S CHAMBER

The room traditionally known as the Queen's Chamber never had anything to do with queens of any kind; the misleading name was bestowed by early Arab explorers and has simply stuck, despite the best efforts of archaeologists to impose a more accurate label. Sited exactly on the Pyramid's central east–west axis, it can be reached by going back up the descending passage until it intersects with the ascending passage, 129 feet (39.3 metres) long, which cuts up into the masonry at an angle of 26 degrees 2 minutes and 30 seconds – almost precisely the same uphill gradient as the descending passage's slope downwards. After climbing up this passage for several minutes – not an easy climb – one reaches another junction, and can either proceed still further upwards or take the softer option of a horizontal passage. It is this passage which leads to the Queen's Chamber.

The corbelled niche in the east wall of the Queen's Chamber was probably intended to contain a *ka* statue of the king.

The chamber measures 18 feet 10 inches (5.7 metres) from east to west and 17 feet 2 inches (5.2 metres) from north to south; it has a pointed or 'pented' roof which rises to 20 feet 5 inches (6.2 metres) at its highest. Cut into the east wall is a sizeable corbelled niche 15 feet 4 inches (4.7 metres) high, 5 feet 2 inches (1.6 metres) wide at the base, and originally 3 feet 5 inches (1 metre) deep, although subsequent visitors have hacked it still deeper. The walls and roof are made from fine limestone but the floor is quite rough, suggesting that it, too, was left in an unfinished state.

When the builders abandoned the Queen's Chamber, they sealed it off completely at the point where the horizontal passage meets the ascending passage. It is this fact, as well as the presence of that corbelled niche, which suggests that the chamber was actually designed as a *serdab* – a room which contained, not the king's body, but a larger-than-lifesize statue representing his *ka*. This term, which is sometimes rendered in English as 'soul' or 'spirit' or 'life force', has no true equivalent; its full complexity will be examined in Chapter 5,

Covering a wide corridor while withstanding the enormous stresses above it, the Grand Gallery is considered an architectural masterpiece.

but in simple terms the *ka* was a kind of belt-and-braces ploy, an insurance policy for the king's post-mortem state. If the royal body itself came to harm, the *ka* statue could replace it. Djoser's *ka* statue was found sealed inside a stone box on the north side of his step pyramid.

THE GRAND GALLERY AND THE KING'S BURIAL CHAMBER

Now, if one returns down the horizontal passage and goes on and up again, the two most dazzling structures within the Great Pyramid can be reached. After a short climb up the ascending passage, at the same angle of just over 26 degrees, suddenly its narrow confines (still only about 3 feet 6 inches or 1 metre wide) open up to a truly astonishing spectacle – one of the most overwhelming achievements of ancient architecture.

The Grand Gallery

Essentially a continuation of the ascending passage – it keeps the same gradient right along its length – the Gallery is a creation on a majestic scale. Fully 153 feet (46.6 metres) long, it rises to a height of 28 feet (8.5 metres), the first 7 feet 6 inches (2.3 metres) of which are vertical walls of fine, highly polished limestone. Above that, seven stone courses mounted one on top of the other rise to the roof, each course jutting out a further 3 inches (7.6 cm) beyond its lower partner; they create a beautiful corbelled vault effect, derived from, but far transcending, the corbelled roof designs found at Meidum and Dahshur.

At the very top, the now narrow space between the two walls (3 feet 5 inches or 1 metre) is spanned by slabs, each one artfully laid in such a way that its weight bears down vertically rather than back along the slope – an arrangement which has kept this apparently precarious structure stable for 4500 years. Along the foot of each wall runs a flat ramp 2 feet (61 cm) high, 1 foot 8 inches (50 cm) wide. Between the two ramps runs a sort of trough, the width of which – 3 feet 5 inches (1 metre) – echoes the slabs of the roofing.

Two final details are worth noting. Along the sides of the gallery are regularly spaced, symmetrically matching holes, cut horizontally into the benches and the walls; there are fifty-six in all, fifty-four of them cut in two rows of twenty-seven, the last two being cut on each side of the high step at the Gallery's upper end. And at the very bottom of the ramp on the western side of the gallery, previously concealed by a stone, is the opening to a shaft or 'well' which plunges perpendicularly into the body of the Pyramid, then forks off at slightly oblique angles before cutting down into the Giza bedrock and emerging in the west wall of the descending passage. More of this shortly.

For the meantime, if one continues to climb up through the Gallery a horizontal opening is eventually reached which leads into the antechamber.

The Antechamber

The south, east and west walls of this space are of red granite. Four large slots have been cut into the east and west walls, three of them running down to the floor and the northernmost, smaller than the others, stopping at the roof of the passage. Passing through this, one finally comes to the spiritual heart of the Great Pyramid.

The granite lined King's Burial Chamber, seen here in a photograph from 1930, contains the now empty and broken sarcophagus of King Khufu.

The King's Burial Chamber

It is a large room, and unexpectedly simple in design. Made of the same red granite as the antechamber, it is 34 feet 4 inches (10.5 metres) from east to west, 17 feet 2 inches (5.2 metres) from north to south and 19 feet 1 inch (5.8 metres) high. Towards the west wall is a lidless rectangular sarcophagus, also of granite: Khufu's resting place. When Flinders Petrie made his study of the chamber, he noticed that this receptacle was about an inch wider than the ascending chamber, and so made the reasonable assumption that it must have been set in position while the chamber was still being built. It is placed on the exact central axis of the Pyramid. Once, it would have been lidded, and contained a wooden coffin, but raiders made off with both corpse and coffin in antiquity. There are clear signs of rough handling – ugly scratch marks from a saw.

Looking upwards, one can see nine great roofing slabs, each well over 18 feet (5.5 metres) long, each estimated as weighing between 25 and 50 tons, which makes the total weight for the whole roof about 400 tons – remarkable. But far more remarkable than the Chamber's visible roof is its set of invisible roofs (see page 141). Mounted one above the other on top of this set of slabs is a series of five separate chambers, the first four taking the form of flat rectangles and the fifth being pointed or pented. It seems clear that the purpose of these hollows was to lessen the load bearing directly down on the King's Chamber and so protect it from caving in. This structure is without precedent anywhere in Egypt, and virtually without parallel.

Large cracks in all of the nine roof slabs and in many of those in the chambers above it suggest that this apparently excessive caution paid off. Recalling how many of the Seven Wonders of the World were destroyed by earthquakes, we can be grateful for the Egyptian skills which ensured that Khufu's Pyramid remained largely unscathed inside as well as outside.

European travellers knew about at least the first of these relieving chambers from the middle of the eighteenth century, and were able to clamber up into it by way of a hole that someone had cut at the top of the east wall – a man called Davidson first mentions this entrance in 1765. It was not until the surveys of Vyse and Perring, though, that anyone managed to hollow out a shaft and climb up into the higher spaces. What the British explorers discovered was a structure made of undressed limestone, installed here fresh from the quarry and daubed with red ochre markings. Among them is a particularly poignant piece of graffiti, which, translated, approximates to 'We did this with pride in the name of our great King Khufu' – using the full term *Khnum-Khuf*. These chambers are the only place in the entire Pyramid where the pharaoh's name is inscribed.

This hidden protective structure almost marks the end of this rapid tour through the inner world. But not quite.

THE DIAGONAL SHAFTS

One small detail of the King's Chamber is as compelling as any of its more obvious architectural feats. In the north and the south walls, about 3 feet (90 cm) from the floor, are single apertures. The northern one is the opening for a long, narrow shaft which runs all the way up to the Pyramid's exterior face at an angle of 31 degrees; the southern runs in the same way, at an angle of 45 degrees. As was soon discovered, the northern shaft is oriented towards the Pole stars; the southern to the constellation of Orion.

The discovery of these shafts set archaeologists wondering: were they paralleled anywhere else? The answer came in 1872, when an engineer named Waynman Dixon made his way around the walls of the Queen's Chamber, tapping and listening, in search of anything hollow. Sure enough he found a pair of shafts, about 8 inches (20 cm) square, which corresponded very closely indeed to the two which ran from the King's Chamber. On the north side, the shaft ran horizontally for 6 feet 4 inches (1.9 metres), then upwards at an angle of about 37 degrees 28 minutes – aimed in the direction of the Pole stars. On the south, the shaft ran horizontally for 6 feet 8 inches (2 metres), then upwards at an angle of 38 degrees 28 minutes – aimed in the direction of Orion.

Diagonal shaft in the north wall of the King's Burial Chamber.

There was, however, one key difference. The shafts from the Queen's Chamber did not reach the outside, but stopped dead as if abandoned. Or were they blocked for some unknown reason? Investigations in the 1990s suggested the latter. A German archaeologist, Rudolf Gantenbrink, sent a small robot camera climbing up the southern shaft of the Queen's Chamber. After about 214 feet (65 metres) it came to a stop, and sent back pictures of a stone plug with two copper pins embedded in it. The purpose of this block, and the nature of what – other

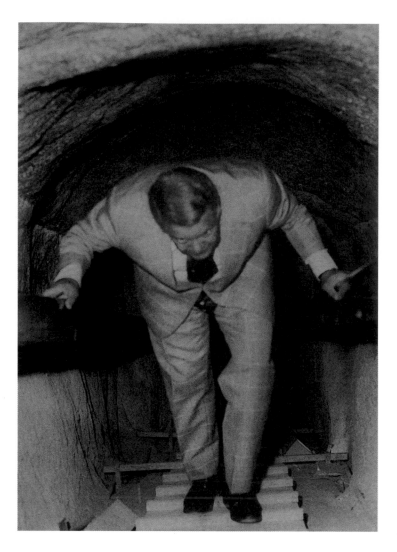

The main entrance of the Great Pyramid was officially reopened in July 1975 by the Egyptian culture minister Youssef el-Sebaei, seen here in the passage down which the coffin of King Khufu had been carried more than 4,500 years earlier.

than masonry – might lie beyond, continue to baffle experts.

But the purpose of the narrow shafts that run from the King's Chamber is now known. They were concerned with religious ritual, and will be examined in Chapter 5.

SEALING THE PYRAMID

Before moving outside, we need to take a second look at two of the sights already noted, this time dwelling on their mechanical function. First, let us look again at those large slots in the walls of the antechamber. What was their purpose? Once again, Petrie played an important part in solving a puzzle, since he found a large fragment of tell-tale red granite in the descending passage and correctly inferred that it had once been part of a portcullis system in the antechamber. Matching pieces of granite were found in the antechamber itself, and are still visible there.

On the day when the Pyramid was finally sealed, the withdrawing priests and workers lowered three large granite slabs, weighing around 2¼ tons, into the slots by means of a rough system of ropes and beams. This was the inner-most line of defence.

Then the party retreated down the Grand Gallery. Do you recall those matching holes cut in the wall? These, we now know, were used for holding in place a series of strong wooden beams, which in turn held up a colossal mass of granite blocks. Why? Because, for all the beauty of its design, the Grand Gallery is very much a functional creation, comparable to the slipway from which a ship is launched into the water, and designed for one ultimate purpose only: to create an impassable seal. The retreating party knocked away the beams which supported those granite plugs, and the plugs tumbled down, blocking the path to the King's Chamber in perpetuity: the second line of defence.

We can imagine that it was an intensely hazardous task, but, contrary to the movies and the folklore, the Egyptians of the Old Kingdom did not go in for sealing up the living with the dead. Our elite group would have made its escape by means of that long shaft running from the bottom west side of the Gallery and all the way down to the descending passage, very close to the point at which it joins the subterranean chamber. Last of all, after climbing back up the descending passage, they plugged everything from the junction of the descending and ascending passages all the way back up to the entrance: the third line of defence. Then they were out into the open air.

The final limestone block of the casing was set in place where the entrance, now blocked, had formerly stood. To the uninstructed eye, this white stone was utterly indistinguishable from any other part of the Pyramid, and the secret of the way in was lost for ever. Or so they believed.

It is not known exactly when raiders first excavated their way into the Pyramid's mysteries. Arab tradition has it that the roughly cut aperture which can now be seen in the north face, not far below the original entrance, was the work of the Caliph Al-Mamun – son of the legendary Harun Al-Rashid from the *Arabian Nights* – who, some time in the late ninth century AD, raided the Pyramid in a fruitless search for hidden treasures (see Chapter 6). But the reality is that the Pyramid had been invaded and looted far, far earlier.

Now it is time to step outside and see the bigger world of which the Pyramid was a part.

The original entrance of the Great Pyramid is in the centre of this picture. The forced entrance made by Al-Mamun and his men (see Chapter 6) is further down and to the right.

OUTSIDE THE PYRAMID: KHUFU'S PYRAMID COMPLEX

SADLY, very little of the wonderful setting for Khufu's creation remains. Happily, what does remain adheres so consistently to architectural patterns discovered at other pyramid sites that we can reconstruct almost all of its appearance with a good deal of accuracy. Here is an account of its principal elements.

THE ENCLOSURE WALL

On completion, the entire Pyramid was closed off around its base by a wall of fine Turah limestone, about 26 feet (8 metres) high. Between the wall and the Pyramid's base was a court, about 33 feet (10 metres) wide, also paved in limestone. The only way into this courtyard was via an entrance in the mortuary temple.

THE MORTUARY TEMPLE

Built opposite the eastern face of the Pyramid, this was a rectangular building measuring roughly 171 feet (52 metres) from north to south and 132 feet (40 metres) from east to west. Made of limestone, with finely detailed relief carvings on the walls, it was connected to the causeway (see page 88) by a door in its own east façade. Much larger than its corresponding temples at the Bent Pyramid and at Meidum, it enclosed an open courtyard paved with black basalt, surrounded by a sort of cloister or colonnade, its roof supported by granite columns – mainly square columns except for those in the corners, which were oblong. A stone stairway at the inside southwest corner provided access to the colonnade's roof.

On the western side of the court was a deep recess which seems to have led to another type of enclosure, possibly for storage rooms, and an inner sanctuary made up of an altar with round-topped stelae (engraved stone columns) on either side, although this interpretation has been disputed. Later mortuary temples point to the likely presence of five statue niches, containing representations of the king, and two false doors on the western wall, but no trace of these has so far been found. The door into the Pyramid court was at the northwest corner.

THE SATELLITE PYRAMID

This small echo of the main building, its sides only 66 feet (20 metres) long at the base, remained undiscovered until relatively recently, when it was turned up by the noted Egyptian archaeologist Zahi Hawass in the course of some routine cleaning exercises. Sited directly to the southeast of the Great Pyramid, and possibly intended as a home for Khufu's *ka*, it has a descending passage in the form of a T and a small burial chamber, the sides of which – like the galleries in Djoser's step pyramid – sag inwards as if mimicking the shape of a tent.

THE BOAT PITS

These structures fall into two main groups: pits dug in the shape of boats, and long, rectangular pits that contain the disassembled parts of real boats. The first group are dispersed around the Pyramid complex, outside the enclosing courtyard. One lies parallel to the causeway, close to the mortuary temple. Two others lie to the north and south of that temple. A fourth lies between two of the queens' pyramids (see below), and a fifth next to the satellite pyramid. The second group was not discovered until May 1954, by another Egyptian archaeologist Kamal el-Mallakh; each of the two pits was covered with huge slabs of limestone. When the dismantled pieces were extracted from the first pit – 1224 pieces in all, varying in size from 75 feet (23 metres) to 4 inches (10 cm) – craftsmen under the eye of the master restorer Hag Ahmed Yusuf discovered that they could be reassembled into a complete boat. The process took them the better part of fourteen years, but at the end of it they had an almost perfect royal Nile vessel of considerable dimensions: 142 feet (43.3 metres) from prow to stern, and with a displacement of 45 tons. It can now be seen by visitors to Giza in its own museum.

The reassembled boat of Khufu, found in 1954.

Computer-generated view of the
Great Pyramid and its site.

KEY

A Great Pyramid

B Enclosure wall

C Mortuary temple

D Satellite pyramid

E Queens' pyramids

F *Mastaba* cemetery

G Causeway

‹------›

Boat pit (concealed)

Inset The Valley Temple on the
west bank of the River Nile.

View down the side of the
Great Pyramid towards the
queens' pyramids.

The esoteric significance of these boats and boat pits will be explored in Chapter 5. Meanwhile, our survey of the complex continues with the queens' pyramids.

THE QUEENS' PYRAMIDS

Khufu built three of these, at right-angles to the upper part of the causeway, on the southeast side of the Great Pyramid. Archaeologists know them by the romantic names of GI-a, GI-b and GI-c; all three once had small chapels, miniature counterparts of Khufu's mortuary temple, though only that of GI-c has survived intact to the present day. Each of the pyramids also has a descending passage, leading to a burial chamber via a sudden turn to the west.

Who were the queens buried here? Herodotus (II, 126) tells a lurid story about the second of the three pyramids:

> The wickedness of Cheops [Khufu] reached to such a pitch that, when he had spent all his treasures and wanted more, he sent his daughter to the stews [brothels], with orders to procure him a certain sum – how much I cannot say, for I was not told; she procured it, however, and at the same time, bent on leaving a monument which should perpetuate her own memory, she required each man to make her a present of a stone towards the works which she contemplated. With these stones she built the pyramid which stands mid-most of the three that are in front of the Great Pyramid, measuring along each side a hundred and fifty feet.

With due deference to the father of all historians, this is nonsense. Although there is no great certainty, the soundest deductions point to the first, northernmost pyramid being intended for Queen Hetepheres; the second for Queen Meritetes; and the third for Queen Henutsen.

Hetepheres was, in all probability, Khufu's mother. At any rate, texts found when the tomb close to this pyramid was opened, in 1925, link her name with that of Khufu's father Sneferu, whose Horus-name *Neb-Maat*, 'Lord of Truth', was handsomely inscribed on the fragments of a canopy; she is referred to not only as 'Daughter of the God' but as 'Mother of the King'; and seal impressions found elsewhere in the tomb refer to *Her-Mejedu* – Khufu's Horus-name. (This tomb, incidentally, is the only cache of royal equipment left even partly intact by thieves. Although damaged, many of its contents are of considerable beauty; the greatest surprise to greet the first explorers was a sealed alabaster box containing the queen's internal organs – a type of vessel known as a canopic, so named after a Greek myth about a sailor called Canopus, who later became identified with Osiris, the Egyptian god of resurrection and hope.)

Meritetes has been identified on the strength of an inscription found in the first *mastaba* to the east, which belongs to Khufu's (supposed) eldest son Kawab. It is known that Meritetes lived long enough to experience at least part of four reigns – those of Sneferu, Khufu, Djedefre and Khafre. It is possible that she was Khufu's queen and Kawab's mother, since it is conjectured that those buried in the *mastabas* closest to the small triad of pyramids were all queens' sons.

Henutsen's connection with the third tomb is based largely on the attribution of much later times – the XXIst Dynasty and later – when she was associated with the goddess Isis and given the honorary name Isis-Mistress-of-the-Pyramid. Almost nothing is known of her, though she may have been Khufu's half-sister.

Immediately to the north of the queens' pyramids ran the causeway.

THE CAUSEWAY

Herodotus claimed that the causeway to the mortuary temple was covered with exceptionally fine relief carvings of animals, and although this account was regarded with scepticism for many years, modern exploration suggests that he was right after all. Recently uncovered fragments of the relief, though few in number, appear to match his description. The foundations of this causeway – sometimes described as a corridor – which ran all the way down to the valley temple, rose to more than 130 feet (40 metres) high at certain points, while in other places it was built directly on the bedrock. Today, the lower end of the causeway disappears beneath the modern town of Kafr es-Samman; substantial excavations were not carried out here until the late 1980s, when archaeologists unearthed not only sections of the causeway foundation and a layer of mud-brick buildings (possibly the *Gerget Khufu*, 'Khufu's settlement', a small town for those who served the Pyramid complex) but all that remained of the valley temple.

THE VALLEY TEMPLE

Sadly, those remains did not constitute much more than some basalt pavings. Although it is almost certain that the temple was an original part of the Pyramid complex, its structure is a matter of conjecture and guesswork. One final point remains.

THE *MASTABA* CEMETERIES

To the east and west of the Great Pyramid's enclosure wall, arranged into parallel rows spaced several feet apart, are two large cemeteries of *mastabas*. Those to the east hold the mortal remains of the king's relatives; the ones to the west, those of his higher officials. Long stripped of their glistening exteriors, these *mastabas* were originally encased in limestone of the same hue as that which coated the Pyramid itself – on the one hand declaring their connection with the king through shared colour and texture, on the other hand expressing their subordination through the massive disparity in scale between *mastabas* and Pyramid.

Our tour of the remains, inside and out, is complete. But before we can go back and see how all these buildings were used at the time of Khufu's funeral, there is one small misconception that must be tidied up.

Tourists on the Giza Sphinx in 1890.

THE GIZA SPHINX

Contrary to popular assumption and myth, the great Giza Sphinx was not the creation of the men who built the Great Pyramid: it was built well after Khufu's death by Khafre (also known as Chephren) as part of his own pyramid complex. Even so, the Sphinx is such a defining part of the Giza plateau as the world now knows it that it deserves a detour.

Khafre, a younger brother of Khufu's short-reigning successor Djedefre (2528–2520 BC) came to the throne in 2520 BC and ruled until 2494 BC. The Sphinx, which stands before Khafre's pyramid as a guard, facing eastwards, was sculpted in the years leading up to c. 2500 BC, and was far and away the largest piece of sculpture Egypt had ever seen. Not for more than a thousand years, and the reigns of Amenhotep III and Ramesses II, would the Egyptians ever create works of art on such a massive scale.

The Sphinx rises to 66 feet (20 metres) at the highest point of its head, and is about 240 feet (73 metres) long from end to end; the face is 13 feet 8 inches (4.2 metres) at its widest point. Its builders carved much of it from the bedrock at the bottom of Khafre's causeway, beginning by digging a large trench in the shape of a U, then cutting a lion's body from the resulting hillock. The stones quarried here were used to build a Sphinx Temple. On completion, it may well have been covered with plaster and decorated with paint.

The varying condition of the Sphinx today reflects the different geological strata from which it was carved: the relatively well-preserved state of the head is due to its being composed of far stronger stone – it lacks a nose, and has all but lost the royal emblem of a beard suspended from the chin, but is still quite recognizable as a human face. Some authorities believe that it may have been planned as an accurate representation of Khafre himself, rather than as a merely formal or abstract image of a man.

Why the body shape of a lion? One reason may be that in Egyptian mythology the lion is frequently a guardian of holy places; another, that the priests of Heliopolis incorporated this ancient belief into their solar cosmology, and made the lion the guardian of the gates of the Underworld to the east and west. Mutated from lion into sphinx by the addition of humanoid features – originally, those of the sun-god Atum – the creature was then pressed into general duty as a tomb guardian. There is also some evidence for a cult belief that the king, after his death, actually became Atum: hence, one reading of the Great Sphinx is that it shows Khafre transfigured into the sun-god. Whether or not this is accurate, few have seriously questioned the view that the symbolic function of the Sphinx is protective.

It is a curious fact that none of the classical authors who give an account of the Giza plateau – Herodotus, Diodorus and Strabo – make any mention of the Sphinx. The most likely explanation is that the Sphinx was often entirely buried beneath wind-blown sand – a possibility which accounts for the fact that it has survived so comparatively well despite the fragility of much of its stone.

With our inner and outer tours complete, we are now much better equipped to understand the full mysteries of Khufu's funeral.

CHAPTER FIVE

DEATH, AFTERLIFE AND THE FUNERAL OF THE KING

2528 BC: KHUFU IS DEAD. This is, in a sense, the great day he has been preparing for ever since he took the throne in his ambitious youth, and became an incarnation of the god Horus. It is also the day which finally gives point to all the colossal expenditure of labour, time, resources and skill at the Giza site over the last two decades and more. For, although fringe 'pyramidologists' seem to feel obliged routinely to pour scorn on a fact that has been well established by countless sound scholars, there is actually one very obvious answer to the question: what is a pyramid? A pyramid is a tomb – a tomb for a king or queen.

Today, we would regard a king, or an immensely rich man, who spent two or three decades of his life and a large part of his fortune on building a colossal tomb as being at best eccentric, at worst frankly insane – gripped by a weird combination of morbidity and megalomania. Even had they dared to entertain such anachronistic, blasphemous thoughts, however, none of Khufu's subjects would have seen anything other than regal dignity, inevitability and fundamental good sense in his actions. Naturally Khufu should wish to express his glory in the greatest human monument of all time: after all, he was pharaoh. Naturally he should spend all his life looking forward to death: after all, he was a god.

THE EGYPTIAN CONCEPT OF THE AFTERLIFE

It has been well said that the popular idea of the ancient Egyptians as a people utterly obsessed by death is the precise opposite of the truth. On the contrary, they were so attached to life that they wished, above all things, to ensure it for ever. In order to grasp the logic of this belief fully, it is necessary to know something about their spiritual assumptions and funeral practices in general: although the importance of a king's death as far exceeds that of a common Egyptian as a pyramid exceeds a mud-brick house, both of them looked up to the same heavens and the same afterlife.

Sadly, many introductory accounts of Egyptian religion produce a state of confusion in the reader, because they tend to scramble together all the many things that the Egyptians were known to have believed at some time or other in the course of three millennia and in different parts of the kingdom where many local deities and cults thrived. For example, we may read that the cult of Osiris – god of resurrection and hope – was of national importance, and that any Egyptian concerned about the afterlife would try if possible to make a pilgrimage to Osiris's festivals at Abydos. Just so: but only in the Middle

Previous page
The *ba*, depicted as a large bird with a human head, hovers over a mummy. Illustration from a New Kingdom *Book of the Dead*.

Kingdom, from the XIIth Dynasty (1991–1783 BC) onwards. At the time of the Old Kingdom, Osiris was still a relatively minor deity.

Nor is the confusion merely the result of conflating three-thousand years of belief into an undifferentiated mass. Frugal housekeepers in spiritual as well as material things, the Egyptians appear to have been reluctant to throw away any belief that had once been serviceable, with the result that mythological narratives of great antiquity sometimes lived on long after new myths had arrived, in a contradictory state that no one seemed to mind. Finally, some of the more refined, metaphysical aspects of Egyptian faith are very hard for those raised with entirely different notions of life, death and the 'soul' to comprehend.

JUDGEMENT OF ONE'S EARTHLY LIFE

Bearing all this in mind, perhaps the most rewarding approach to understanding the full implications of Khufu's death and burial is to see what the king had in common with his people in the face of mortality, and in what ways he was entirely unique.

First, it seems that every Egyptian, high or low, anticipated an afterlife which would involve a process of judgement. Wellbeing in the next life depended on one's conduct in the present life, and specifically to having adhered to *maat* – a complex notion encompassing individual morality, social law, the physical make-up of the universe and its deep underlying logic and harmony. It included the rigidly hierarchical idea of right action appropriate to one's social status: those who aspired to rise above their origins might easily stand accused of transgressing their *maat*.

According to one text, all the deeds of a man's life, both in accord with and in wicked defiance of *maat*, are piled up in a heap beside him, and remain by him for all eternity. Hence the formula found on many funeral inscriptions, asserting and listing all the dead person's claims to clement treatment, and beginning with the ritual insistence: 'I spoke *maat*, I did *maat* ...'

Although this IVth Dynasty limestone head with its wig of curly hair has been in the collection of the Berlin Museum for more than a century, it has only recently been identified as representing Khufu.

THE PRESERVATION OF THE BODY

Second, as is well known, the Egyptians had a much more fleshly concept of posthumous life than many cultures, and set great store by the protection of dead bodies. Every Egyptian who could afford one would arrange to have a tomb built, usually at the edge of the western desert – the land of the dead, where the sun set. The standard tomb was either cut into the side of a cliff, or made of stone blocks. This latter kind was almost always divided into two parts: an underground chamber, dug as deeply as was economically possible below the ground, entered by means of a shaft, and containing both the dead person and all relevant funerary trappings; and a sort of chapel above, where the family and priests could carry out the necessary rites for the dead.

Such tombs were often adorned with hair-raising threats about the vengeance that would be visited on anyone who dared to break into the tomb. It is this practice which lies behind the spooky idea, much beloved by Hollywood, of ancient Egyptian curses, and particularly of the supposed 'curse of Tutankhamun' which once helped sell so many newspapers.

To be sure, only a very few Egyptians of the higher social orders could ever afford tombs on such a grand scale. Humbler folk would have to be content with a simple pit, dug in cemetery grounds near the great *mastabas*; while the poorest of all were sometimes rolled up in mats, provided with a few simple clay vessels, and laid on the ground.

The significance placed on a good solid tomb was matched only by the care devoted to mummification – a practice initially reserved for the very highest ranks of Egyptian society, but which grew more widespread as well as more technically advanced over the centuries, so that by the first millennium BC it was a fairly common practice. It began, it is assumed, from the observation that bodies buried directly in sand would dehydrate so rapidly that the normal processes of decomposition would hardly have time to begin, and all the organs would be preserved, shrivelled but intact.

Improving on nature, the Egyptians then experimented with various wrappings, coated with resin to improve the preservative effect. Some time towards the end of the IIIrd Dynasty, around 2600 BC, they also began ritually to dissect their dead, placing the more fragile organs in containers – often jars, known to archaeologists as canopic vessels – where they were sealed up until such time as the deceased might need them again.

The remainder of the body was then subjected to an accelerated drying

Opposite
Although few Old Kingdom mummies have survived, by the New Kingdom embalming techniques had improved sufficiently to ensure that many bodies from that period would remain remarkably intact to the present day. Examination of the mummy of Ramesses II, for example, has revealed that he lived to be over eighty (an unusually old age), walked with a limp and suffered from arthritis, abscesses on his teeth and hardening of the arteries. He died around 1212 BC and is thought by some to be the pharaoh referred to in the book of Exodus.

process using a substance known as natron, whose active ingredient was sodium carbonate; it was wrapped in bandages and then treated to certain funeral rituals, which will be examined in greater detail below. But the technology of mummification was not very far advanced in the Old Kingdom; very few bodies have survived in any form approximating to a true mummy. It was not until the New Kingdom (1550–1070 BC, a good thousand years after Khufu's death) that the Egyptians developed anything like an adequate mummification technique, although it remained a major concern of their culture at all times.

ESSENTIALS FOR THE AFTERLIFE

The third and last major idiosyncrasy of Egyptian death practices is the set of beliefs which provide a logic both to their funerals and to their mortuary cults of the dead. Since cemeteries were located to the west, the process of taking the body to its resting place would often involve crossing of the Nile by barge; but this practical necessity was also charged with obvious symbolic significance, since the passage across water from east to west was also the passage from life to death. On the same barge, or just behind it on an accompanying boat, would be a statue – the *ka* statue – showing what the dead person had looked like in their youth. Should the actual body come to some harm, the statue could provide an acceptable substitute for future life.

Once the sarcophagus had reached the burial chamber, it would be solemnly surrounded with all the necessities for a full posthumous existence – the canopic vessels and their assorted organs, food, clothing, jewels and objects indicative of high or regal status, toiletries and assorted oils. In the Middle Kingdom small human figures called *ushabtis* were entombed with the deceased to carry out any manual labour that might be required of the dead person by the gods. By way of back-up for all these essentials, the sarcophagus was often decorated with similar objects – clearly the gods drew no very sharp distinction

Top In the Middle Kingdom Egyptians buried their dead with *ushabtis* – miniature worker figures that would enable the deceased to answer the gods' call to work. Hundreds were found in this excavation at Saqqara in 1949.

Above The lids of canopic jars were sometimes shaped to represent the four sons of Horus: the baboon-headed Hapi (for the lungs), the human-headed Imseti (the liver), the jackal-headed Duamutef (the stomach) and the falcon-headed Qebekh-sennuef (the intestines).

between things and their depictions, so that a painting of food might be just as nourishing as the real thing.

But perhaps the single most striking of all Egyptian funeral practices was the one which began after the burial itself. Even today other cultures observe periods of mourning, and may mark anniversaries of the dead person's departure, but the ancient Egyptians believed that their duties were far more taxing than such intermittent observance. The dead had to be constantly provided for throughout the months, years, even centuries after their passage to the next world. Food had to be brought to the tomb or mortuary chapel on a regular basis, and the names of these foods were to be spoken out loud to ensure their efficacy. A caste of priests, the *ka* servants, would ensure the continuity and propriety of rituals at the chapel – contracted in the deceased's lifetime and binding for generations of priests to come, much as modern-day contractual agreements between corporations or states may long outlast the individual representatives who first drew them up.

In the case of kings, such services were on a grand scale. The temple of the Vth Dynasty King Neferirkare-Kakai at Abusir reveals that something like thirty people were kept in full-time employment, both in bringing food supplies to the dead and performing the rites and in providing support services as cooks, builders, porters and launderers. (Since the 'consumption' of food by the dead was not visible to mortal eyes, the workers were, it seems, allowed to take offerings home at the end the day for their own families.) The services at Neferirkare-Kakai's temple continued for well over two hundred years, and possibly much longer.

Such was the typical way of death for Egyptians of high rank. Khufu's funeral and mortuary cult are broadly similar to this general pattern; but since he was king, the responsibilities which devolved upon his priesthood were vastly more awe-inspiring. And the nature of his tomb was vastly more magical.

KHUFU'S FUNERAL

It has already been suggested that one way for modern readers to contemplate the Pyramid might be to regard it as a machine for the dead. This metaphor can be justified in an obvious, practical sense, for the building did contain a number of ingenious contrivances: think of the portcullis mechanisms in the antechamber to the King's Burial Chamber, or the system of wooden beams and stone plugs

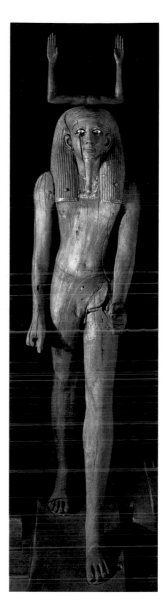

The life-size wooden *ka* statue of King Hor, which dates from about 1780 BC and was found standing in his tomb at Dahshur.

held ready for final deployment in the Grand Gallery, all designed to ensure the perpetual safety of the royal remains. But the metaphor also applies in more precise and spiritual ways: remember, for example, those curious narrow shafts running out from the King's Chamber, pointed at significant stars, whose metaphysical purpose will be examined shortly. Moreover, our 'machine' metaphor can be extended from the Pyramid itself to the king's funeral rites, which were in essence an extended part of the total pyramid mechanism.

Modern knowledge of what happened at Khufu's funeral is at once fragmentary and conjectural, derived partly from the material testimony of the site itself, partly from information gleaned in other tombs. None of the tomb decorations found so far directly represents either Khufu's funeral or that of any other king. The details available derive from accounts of how various high officials were buried at the time, brought together with texts that unfold Egyptian religious beliefs about royalty and some of their other ritual practices.

Among the most important of the sources are the so-called pyramid texts. The first of these was discovered in 1881 by the brothers Emile and Heinrich Brugsch while investigating the pyramids of Unas, Teti, Pepi I, Merenre and Pepi II – pyramids, that is, from the very end of the Vth Dynasty (up to 2323 BC) and throughout the VIth (2323–2150 BC). Pyramid texts are now known to be extracts from a very old corpus of Egyptian religious writings, and their main theme is the king's eternal existence. As one might expect, there is considerable repetition from tomb to tomb, much as the inscriptions in Christian churches often quote identical passages from the Bible or standard prayers. Well over seven hundred basic pyramid texts have been found and translated, and it is from those which clearly refer to such ritual actions as the introduction of equipment to the king's grave that much of our relevant knowledge is derived.

As explained earlier, Egyptian burial rites combined all the functions of mourning and social cohesion familiar from other cultures with a number of highly idiosyncratic features. Some, again, provided what they saw as basic practical necessities for the progress of the deceased into healthy posthumous being – such as 'feeding' the dead person on a regular basis. Others reflected complex – and to later eyes, sometimes contradictory – beliefs about the nature of the universe, both visible and invisible.

Major Egyptian funeral ceremonies were divided and subdivided into as few as four and as many as sixteen different sections. Khufu's, beyond doubt one of the grandest ever, may well have been of unexampled complexity. None the less, it would have been based on several crucial components.

PREPARATION OF THE BODY

For many members of the Egyptian elite, body preparation was something which usually happened prior to the crucial symbolic phase of the river journey. In later dynasties, the period between death and burial was established as seventy days, but it seems that in the Old Kingdom this could have been much longer – in the case of the IVth Dynasty Queen Meresankh III, a full 272 days. Some kind of preparation of Khufu's body may have taken place well before his funeral, then; but evidence suggests that his body was actually prepared after his ceremonial river journey. So let us begin at his residence – probably his palace at Memphis, very shortly after his death.

FROM THE HOUSE TO THE RIVER

The coffin was brought out on a bier (a frame). Professional female mourners dressed in long white robes howled and wailed; beside and behind them other anguished mourners – male and female – hurled themselves into the dust and writhed, tearing their clothes into shreds. In the time of the Old Kingdom, the procession was led by a woman known as the Kite – either the widow of the great man, or a professional mourner. In later periods, when the cult of Osiris had become more prominent, a second Kite role was introduced: the two were held to represent Isis and Nephthys, divine mourners of Osiris.

An attendant awaits the arrival of Khufu's funeral barge at the Valley Temple. (Reconstruction)

Other essential participants included the *Wet* (literally 'the Wrapper'), who was the Chief Embalmer – also known as the Seal-Bearer of the God – charged with the task of transforming the mortal remains into a mummy. The Lector Priest, or 'He Who Carries the Ritual', was entrusted with the parallel task of spiritual transformation: he bore the scroll of requisite magical utterances, used for the early stages of turning the dead man into an *akh* – the term, discussed below, may for now be translated as 'appropriately blessed spirit'.

THE RIVER JOURNEY

The Lector Priest pours holy water over the pharaoh's coffin.

It is not known for certain whether Khufu died, so to speak, in his own home – the royal palace at Memphis. (It has been argued that the entire court may have decamped to a temporary residence at Giza for the duration of the building of the Great Pyramid, although some writers have objected that the noise and inconvenience of living right next door to the world's largest building site was unlikely to have suited royal tastes.) If he did die to the east of the Nile, then the river journey was, as for many of his subjects, a necessity; if not, a passage by water may have been no more than a ritual obligation - perhaps Khufu's barge only made a brief and emblematic journey on one of the canals built around the Giza harbour.

It seems close to certain that the two boats uncovered from long, narrow pits (see Chapter 4) were the actual ones used in Khufu's funeral, carefully dismantled after arrival. One plausible conjecture is that the first boat carried Khufu's body, and the second his *ka* statue. It is also likely that, as the boats sailed along the Nile, the Lector Priest read aloud from his scroll passages from what we now call the pyramid texts.

FROM THE RIVER TO THE TOMB

The funeral boat docked at the pyramid harbour and the dead king was disembarked in front of a structure known as the Doors of Heaven. If his body had already been treated by the *Wet*, it could proceed towards the Pyramid. If not, it could not be allowed to enter the necropolis unpurified, and so would have been taken to an *Ibu en Waab* – a Tent of Purification. This was probably a temporary structure, made of wooden poles and reed mats arranged into a rectangular shape and shielding the procedures within from profane eyes. From the *Ibu* the body was taken on to the *Wabet* – a word which, though literally meaning 'pure', is usually translated as 'mortuary workshop'. Was this part of the mortuary temple? Possibly, although it may also have been an entirely separate building, temporary or permanent – a VIth Dynasty relief shows a *Wabet* made up of three large rooms, a magazine (store room) and a long corridor.

We know what happened in these two structures: partial dismemberment and desiccation of the corpse. We are less sure exactly where these took place, or what length of time was required. Probably the most plausible interpretation is

Pall bearers carry Khufu's coffin to the tomb.

that the body had its brain and other inner organs removed in the *Ibu* and that the remaining mass was taken to the *Wabet* to be dried for a period of seventy days.

If Khufu's evisceration followed the classic pattern, his liver, lungs, stomach and intestines were reverently extracted from an incision made on the lower left side of his torso. Then they were solemnly washed and packed in natron to dry before being stored in canopic vessels, each one supposedly guarded by its own particular god. (In later generations, the dried organs would be packed back into the body cavity.) The heart was left inside, as it was believed to be the centre of feeling and thought. Khufu's brain would have been removed by way of his nostrils, once the servants had broken his ethmoid bone. This, too, would be cleaned, dried and put in elegant storage.

Once safely eviscerated and drained, the body could proceed westward in state towards the tomb – mounted on a sledge, and pulled by oxen. The Kite or Kites rejoined the body here, as did the priests, and the procession was completed by men bearing large quantities of valuable goods – all the usual afterlife requirements, but on an exceedingly grand scale, and probably including tools and weapons alongside the mandatory food, oils and clothing. The transport oxen may also have been sacrificed at the end of the procession, to add plenty of protein to the eternal food store.

The procession passed up the causeway, through the mortuary temple and so, at long last, into the Pyramid.

THE TOMB SERVICE

How many accompanied the king at this stage of his final journey? Texts from the VIth Dynasty specify a figure of eighty men 'allowed' to be in the Burial Chamber, but does not state whether all of them were required to be present at the same time. The relatively modest scale of the King's Chamber suggests that, once all the goods had been unpacked, there would have been room for only a few attendants. The king was gently lowered into his red granite sarcophagus. At least two of the rituals which now took place are known.

The first was the Invocation Offering, or 'Coming Forth at the Voice', in which the dead king was invited to come and enjoy all the offerings that had just been loaded into his tomb, as well as all those which were to come. (Some funeral texts mention the sacrifice of oxen at about this stage of the ritual.) The second ritual was the Opening of the Mouth, a magical procedure mainly involving the use of spoken spells, and calculated to permit the king to breathe, eat and speak in his afterlife. The heavy lid of the sarcophagus was put in place. The final rite was Bringing the Foot – ceremonially brushing the Chamber clean and offering libations.

The funeral party withdrew and the three antechamber portcullises were lowered. The party processed back down into the Grand Gallery and, as we have seen, then closed it by knocking away the wooden supports of giant stone plugs. They made their escape from the Pyramid by means of the vertical shaft and then, after filling in the descending passage with masonry, put the last of the casing stones in place, sealing up the Pyramid for eternity.

Then the real work began, a job which would last for centuries to come. The ritual which had taken place in the King's Chamber was, in a way, as much of an

Above Khufu's red granite sarcophagus in the King's Burial Chamber; empty, lidless and chipped at the corner.

Khufu's coffin is hauled up the ramp to the entrance of the Great Pyramid.

inaugural ceremony for Khufu's death cult as it was the formal closure of his earthly life. Day after day, a group of ritual technicians now had the weighty responsibility of performing the ceremonies that would keep the king alive in the next world, providing him with both material goods and magical incantations.

What, then, did did they think would happen to the king in the next world? To answer that, we need to examine Khufu's funeral and his tomb in the fuller context of Egyptian religion.

THE EGYPTIAN TRINITY: *KA, BA* AND *AKH*

The term *ka* has already been briefly defined as 'soul', 'spirit' or 'life force', but this is somewhat misleading since it asks a word derived from one culture's metaphysics to do work for which it is poorly qualified. The hieroglyph for *ka* shows two arms, bent at the elbows and raised in the air, and is meant to evoke an embrace; the word *ka* itself embraces many shades of meaning. It is, for example, something handed down from one's parents, grandparents and ancestors, like spiritual DNA, traceable in the very remote past to a creator god by way of lesser deities. And the *ka* of a king is the collective life force of all his subjects – crucial to their wellbeing, indeed to their very existence.

But *ka* is also something which can be separated from the individual and exist as a sort of collective *élan vital* or diffuse life force. At the immediate point of death, the *ka* departs from the body and rejoins a broader stream of vital energy while the body is being eviscerated and mummified. The first major posthumous task facing the recently dead king, then, is to set off in search of his absentee *ka* and effect a reunion. This quest is carried out not by the dried and wrapped material remains but by another aspect of the dead monarch – the *ba*.

Ba, to add to the confusion, is also sometimes translated as 'soul', though it can also mean a hybrid of reputation, status, prestige, personality, character and/or fame. Unlike any of these terms, however, the *ba* was not simply an abstraction or a concept but could also be an actual, living thing capable of movement, eating and even the act of sex. Gods had *bas*, in the form of natural phenomena or objects; oddly, objects could also have *bas*.

From these complexities emerges at least one clear idea: that after death the *ba* – represented in a famous New Kingdom *Book of the Dead* illustration as a large bird with human features – had a crucial task to perform, and it could not even begin that task if the deceased's body had been allowed to decay; hence the immense importance of mummification. In the course of a king's funeral, his *ba* would be firmly re-established by dressing his remains (temporarily reduced by mummification to a regrettably anonymous, prematurely democratic likeness of the lowliest peasant) in signs of authority, including all kingly insignia.

The next stage was the most important of all. The king now ascended to the realm of the stars, presided over by the sky goddess Nut. Indeed, he now literally became a star. Once among the stars, the king was transfigured into a third and ultimate mode of being, the *akh*. This astral journey was made possible by the work done back in the Pyramid, by the celebrants of the burial ritual which formally reunites the *ka* and the *ba*. The *akh*, again, is conceived of as an entirely distinct entity, capable of surveying the earth and even intervening in human affairs.

Hence the king lives on in three distinct ways: as *ka*, *ba* and *akh*. (Those who find it hard to assimilate this curious idea might find it helpful to recall the Christian idea of the Trinity.) As explained earlier, the Great Pyramid was called Khufu's *Akhet* – his 'horizon', but the similarity to the word *akh* is more

Above left The glyph of *ka*. Relief detail from the White Chapel of Senusret I, *c.* 1872 BC.

Above right The *akh*, represented as a crested ibis. Relief, *c.* 1250 BC.

than a coincidence, for most of the pyramid names that have come down to modern times allude to the place where transformation from mortal remains to immortal being took place. So though we are fully justified in saying that a pyramid is a king's tomb, we must recognize that for Egyptians a royal tomb was much more than a place where remains were kept. It was the king's gateway to the stars – a launch-pad to the afterlife.

It seems increasingly certain that the pyramid's structure was either symbolically expressive of this central function, or designed to serve it practically – perhaps both. One modern theory suggests that the pyramid derived its shape from observations of the sun's rays as they cut down in a triangular wedge through gaps in cloud formations. This seems plausible: from the time of Sneferu's rule, the solar deity became more and more important to Egyptian religion, and the pyramid texts state that the sun's rays can be used as ramps by means of which the king can ascend to heaven. According to this reading, the pyramid was regarded as the immaterial made material: light into stone.

A competing theory of the pyramid as solar symbol suggests that it may have echoed a primal act of creation. The sun god had three aspects: Khepri (the scarab or dung beetle) in the morning, Re at noon and Atum in the evening. Atum was also the oldest of the creating deities: in the beginning, says one creation story, Atum masturbated and his fallen seed gave rise to Shu, god of air, and Tefnut, goddess of moisture. The principle of order came in the universe.

This moment of cosmic propagation was echoed in the mound which rose out of the abysmal waters of formlessness at the beginning of time: so, the pyramid may symbolize the primeval mound emerging from chaos.

Whatever the precise truth, the pyramid texts leave us in no doubt about the heart of the matter, which was that the king ascended to the stars. And this is almost certainly the explanation of those intriguing narrow passages cut from the King's Chamber and pointing towards Orion in one direction and the Pole stars in the other: in both literal and figurative terms they are the channels up which Khufu would pass to join the 'Indestructibles', and be set among the stars.

The exact details of this royal space travel vary from source to source: he might fly with the wisdom god Thoth (who took the concrete form of an ibis), or climb a ladder, or ride on the back of the dung beetle sun god, Khepri, or simply fly in his own right. The journey was fraught with dangers and oddities to rival anything in Dante's *Inferno*. He would meet a ferryman with his head turned back-to-front, and be forced to recite a self-defensive spell to cross the afterworld lake. He would have his passage barred by female apes ready to chop off his head, and have to deploy a special spell: 'O you apes who cut off heads, I will escape from you ...' Eventually, though, he would arrive in triumph at one of the many heavenly kingdoms, where he would be purified, fed, robed and crowned anew, and could then rule, just as he did on earth, but on an immeasurably more imposing scale.

Although the circumstances of the astral journey vary, the irreducible belief at the core of all of them is that the king rose to the heavens and ruled there. In the words of one pyramid text:

[Chorus:]
Here comes the ascender, here comes the ascender!
Here comes the climber, here comes the climber!
Here comes he who flew up, here comes he who flew up!

[King:]
I ascend upon the thighs of Isis
I climb up upon the thighs of Nephthys
My father Atum seizes my hand for me
And he assigns me to those excellent and wise gods,
The imperishable stars.

Meanwhile, back on earth, the king's son and heir – now confirmed as the new incarnation of Horus – would celebrate his father's cosmic promotion:

> *My father ascends to the sky among the gods ...*
> *He stands as the Great Polar Region,*
> *and learns the speech of the sun-folk ...*

KEEPING CHAOS AT BAY

It is by studying the beliefs enshrined in the pyramid texts that we can finally begin to grasp why it was that Khufu should care so much about his tomb. Underlying the bewildering profusion of Egyptian religion and mythology are a few very simple notions about universal order. The world had been created from chaos, and was under constant threat of lapsing back into chaos. The only way for mankind to hold that horror at bay was by unremitting observance of *maat* – law, correctness, harmony; and the earthly champion of that eternal struggle was the king.

When the king died, the foundations of existence itself were momentarily put in jeopardy, for he was the mortal/god who maintained all the rites and ceremonies which hold reality together. Unless the requirements of *maat* were carried out, so that the king could safely ascend to the heavens and his heir become the new (Horus) god on earth, chaos would flood back into creation and universal darkness would bury all.

Finally, then, some of the definitions used in earlier chapters can be refined. What is a pyramid? A pyramid is a machine for turning a king into a god. Why did the Egyptians go to so much trouble to build the Great Pyramid? They did it to prevent the whole of creation from coming to an end.

CHAPTER SIX

TRAVELLERS' TALES

THE CLASSICAL PERIOD

EARLY EGYPTIAN 'TOURISTS'

THE FIRST 'strangers' to visit the pyramids were Egyptians themselves – although of a much later date than the IVth Dynasty. Flinders Petrie estimated that the monuments were first raided some time during the civil wars which raged from the VIIth to the Xth Dynasties: around 2150–2040 BC. It was at this time, he asserted, that the sealed entrance to the Great Pyramid – its approximate whereabouts probably still known in popular tradition – was torn open, the various levels of plugs, masonry and other obstructions removed and Khufu's chamber violated and stripped bare. By the beginning of the XIIth Dynasty (1991–1783 BC), the Pyramid was already being quarried for the building of a smaller pyramid at Lisht.

But this almost contemptuous attitude towards the past eventually gave way to curiosity, and even reverence. Assorted graffiti show that by the time of the New Kingdom (1550–1070 BC) visits of a more benign nature, akin to early tourism, had made the great monuments of the IIIrd and IVth Dynasties the object of regular resort. The step pyramid of Djoser at Saqqara still bears the name of an otherwise unsung visitor – 'Ahmose, Son of Iptah' – who took it into his head to carry out a trifling act of vandalism. The Giza Sphinx became a particular place of pilgrimage; and later still, by the time of the XXVIth Dynasty (664–525 BC), attempts were even made to revive the plateau as a religious centre, albeit one based on highly inaccurate notions of what Khufu and Khafre had themselves done.

THE ARRIVAL OF THE GREEKS

More substantial written records only begin much later, with the Greeks. Egypt became a Greek possession in 332 BC, after Alexander's conquest of the country, and remained under the rule of the Ptolemies for almost three hundred years until the Roman conquest of 30 BC. There had almost certainly been Greek visitors well before the conquest: according to one rumour, the philosopher Thales travelled there in the sixth century BC, and astonished his guides by being able accurately to calculate the Great Pyramid's height – measuring its shadow at the time of day when his own shadow was equal in length to his height.

In certain respects, the curiosity felt by the Greeks for this novel acquisition anticipates the Northern European craze for all things Egyptian which followed the French invasion at the end of the eighteenth century, and had already been gathering force for a couple of hundred years. Some of the writings which reflect this interest are known to have been destroyed, along with all the other literary riches of the ancient world, when the great library of Alexandria burned – destroyed, along with the adjacent Temple of Serapis, by a Christian mob on the orders of the Emperor Theodosius in AD 389. (It had already suffered major damage before, in the time of Julius Caesar.) Among the authors whose accounts of the Pyramid have been obliterated or have survived only in scraps and tatters are Alexander Polyhistor, Antisthenes, Apion, Artemidorus of Ephesus, Aristagoras, Butoridas, Demetrius of Phaleron, Demoteles, Duris of Samoa, Dionysus of Helicarnassus, Euhumerus ....

Perhaps the gravest loss of all is the thirty volume *Ægyptiaca* or *History of Egypt*, said to have been commissioned by Ptolemy I from a priest, Manetho, and estimated to have been written some time around 250 BC. Something of the content of his burnt pages is known thanks to surviving commentaries on his work from later periods, by writers such as Josephus (end of the first century AD), Africanus (third century AD) and Eusebius (fourth century AD). It is in accordance with Manetho's system that we still divide the history of Egypt into thirty or thirty-one Dynasties; and it is to Josephus that we owe the origins of the popular belief that the Hebrews had been forced into slave labour on the pyramids during their Egyptian exile; a claim that is not merely inaccurate, but inaccurate by well over a thousand years.

Herodotus, author of the most valuable classical description of the Great Pyramid.

HERODOTUS

The earliest full account of the pyramids is the work of Herodotus, known by many (following the verdict of the Roman statesman and orator Cicero) as 'the father of History' and by more sceptical readers (following his successor and rival, Plutarch) as 'the father of Lies'. Born in Helicarnassus, Herodotus arrived in Egypt some time around 450 BC, well primed for his trip by having read all the accounts of the country then available.

The great general theme of his works, today usually called the *Historis* although his own word for them was closer to 'researches', was the relationship between 'Europe' – by which he mainly meant Greece – and the known regions of Africa and Asia. Like a good journalist, Herodotus asked questions of everyone he met on his travels, and, whenever possible, examined important sites with his own eyes. The resulting work is a curious mixture of near-scientific accuracy and utter nonsense, for – although he does not seem to have made anything up on his own account, and could be hard-headed enough at times – he was still inclined to treat his informants uncritically, and repeat their wildest assertions incautiously.

Herodotus's account of Egypt was drawn on in Chapter 2; it remains an invaluable source of information, but only if handled with appropriate care. He begins his account of the Great Pyramid, for instance, with one of the most doubtful of all his assertions:

> Till the death of Rhampsinitus, the priests said, Egypt was excellently governed, and flourished greatly; but after him Cheops [Khufu] succeeded to the throne, and plunged into all manner of wickedness. He closed the temples, and forbade the Egyptians to offer sacrifice, compelling them instead to labour, one and all, in his service. Some were required to drag blocks of stone down the Nile from the quarries in the Arabian range of hills; others received the blocks after they had been conveyed in boats across the river, and drew them to the range of hills called the Libyan ....

This passage is, of course, the origin of the libel that the Pyramid was built by slave labour. From what we know of Herodotus's methods as a writer, there is not much reason to doubt that he was quoting accurately what he had been told; sadly, he was being told a lot of old wives' tales. There is no other evidence that Khufu was any worse a ruler than his predecessors, nor that Egypt suffered under his reign, and there is certainly no corroboration of the wild tale that when Khufu's funds ran low he sent his daughter off to work as a prostitute (see page 87).

Herodotus's version of the Pyramid's structure and dimensions, as seen in earlier chapters, is reasonably accurate. His description of its method of construction, while not quite in line with latest thought, correctly emphasizes that it was constructed in steps and required a giant ramp. And his estimate that it took 'a hundred thousand men' twenty years to complete the structure may contain a grain of truth if this is regarded as a confused report of the (much more likely) figure of one hundred thousand men in any given year, working in four three-monthly shifts of about twenty-five thousand at a time. The one genuinely mysterious reference is to 'the underground chambers, which Cheops intended as vaults for his own use: these last were built on a sort of island, surrounded by water introduced from the Nile by a canal'. Most explorers of the Giza plateau have regarded this detail as myth, or as a garbled folk memory of the Pyramid's subterranean chamber. In recent years, however, it has proved a boon to mystics and other 'alternative' writers (see Chapter 9) who claim that the entire necropolis is riddled with underground tunnels, secret chambers and all sorts of thrilling occult matter. These enthusiasts have yet to uncover anything which impresses the scientific and scholarly communities, but hope springs eternal.

Few of the classical writers who followed in Herodotus's path add greatly to his account, although some offer dry, precise, first-hand accounts which are well worth reading – nevertheless, even the most sober are not wholly credible. Diodorus Siculus, a contemporary of Julius Caesar in the mid-first century BC, suffered from Herodotus's vice of scrambling together things he had read, or had heard, with things that he had actually witnessed, and suffered from the vice to a worse degree. Nor did he have Herodotus's redeeming scepticism: he believed, for example, the stories he was told about rats being spontaneously generated from Nile mud. It was Diodorus who reported that the Great Pyramid's limestone casing had remained 'complete and without the least decay' – a doubtful assertion.

Strabo wrote of Khufu's Pyramid having a movable entrance.

STRABO

The next commentator of major importance was Strabo, who made a trip along the Nile about half a century later, around 24 BC. By this period, Egypt was a province of the Roman Empire. His forty-seven-volume *History*, which may well have contained a comprehensive account of Giza, has not survived; all that remains is the work which, despite its considerable length, is in the nature of an appendix. Strabo's account is mainly cool and scientific; in fact, his *Geographica* is so precise that it was used by the Frenchman Auguste Mariette (see page 144) as a helpful guide in his nineteenth-century excavations at Saqqara. Sadly, Strabo's description of the Pyramid is quite brief, and notable mainly for an interesting detail unmentioned by any other classical source, that of a movable stone entrance to the descending passage of the Great Pyramid – 'a stone that may be taken out, which being raised up, there is a sloping passage'.

This account was taken seriously by the nineteenth-century British archaeologist Flinders Petrie, who had noticed some pivot holes in a corresponding part of the Bent Pyramid at Dahshur, and drew a diagram showing how it might have worked. If it did indeed exist, this trap door would almost certainly have been a very late addition, provided, perhaps, for Greek and Roman tourists. Strabo describes the descending passage as running 374 feet (114 metres) into a vermin-ridden pit – the Subterranean Chamber – whose ceiling was daubed with initials written with smoky torches, suggesting that this was a popular excursion for those Romans rich enough to make it.

PLUTARCH AND PLINY THE ELDER

One of the most interesting contributions to the developing story is that of another major historian, Plutarch (whose *Lives* were the source of Shakespeare's Roman plays), in the first century AD. Plutarch, profoundly hostile to Herodotus, wrote a long essay entitled 'On the Malice of Herodotus', in which he accused his predecessor of many crimes, not the least of which was being 'philobarbarous': that is, too keen by half on those dreadful non-Greeks. It is an early instance of a cultural split, which persists even in modern times, between those who like to play down the genius of the ancient Egyptians and those who like to exaggerate it. Another key representative of the anti-Egyptian camp was Plutarch's contemporary Pliny the Elder, whose *Natural History* (XXXVI), was positively snobbish about the vulgarity of the Giza enterprise: 'We will mention also cursorily the Pyramids, which are in the same country of Egypt – that idle and foolish exhibition of royal wealth. For the cause most assigned for their construction is an intention on the part of those kings to exhaust their treasures, rather than leave them to successors or plotting rivals, or to keep the people from idleness.'

Top Plutarch depicted in a crayon engraving by Tucher, 1837.

Above **Pliny the Elder**

THE CHRISTIAN CULTURAL REVOLUTION

The classical period of writings on Egypt in general and the pyramids in particular dwindled away as Rome's power declined. A line may be drawn under ancient

Egyptian history itself in AD 312, when the Emperor Constantine converted to Christianity, which meant that Egypt became a Christian province of the Empire and would remain so for three centuries. From that date right up to today, one of the most tenacious of all legends repeated about the ancient Egyptians is that they were in possession of some great secret knowledge – a *prisca sapientia* – which had become lost. In one very specific sense, this is obviously true: the Egyptians – or at least their elite classes – knew how to read hieroglyphs.

But the Coptic Christians who now controlled Egypt set about the destruction of their pagan ancestors' remains with a ferocity to rival that of fundamentalist movements of later centuries, from the iconoclasts of the European Reformation to the Taliban of early twenty-first-century Afghanistan. So thorough and unremitting was their cultural purge that they all but wiped out any chance of recovering clues to interpreting that writing. For a millennium and a half, until the breakthrough of the Frenchman Jean-François Champollion, there was not a single person who could read the language of what had been one of the world's greatest civilizations.

FROM THE DARK AGES
TO THE ENLIGHTENMENT

AL-MAMUN'S BREACH

THE NEXT GROUP OF INVADERS WERE THE ARABS, who conquered Egypt in AD 642 and began their own researches and fabrications. It was here, some scholars now maintain, that the first quiet stirrings of the European Renaissance also began. Driven partly by the practical need to build a full-scale military fleet and master navigation – a skill which incorporates astronomy, geography and mathematics, among other disciplines – and partly by more disinterested curiosity, the Arabs set about translating everything they could find on those subjects from Greek writers such as Plato, Aristotle, Euclid and Galen.

One of the key figures in this intellectual revival was Abdullah Al-Mamun, son of the Caliph Harun Al-Rashid from the *Arabian Nights*, who was admiringly portrayed in Gibbon's *Decline and Fall of the Roman Empire* as 'a prince of rare

learning who could assist with pleasure and modesty at the assemblies and disputations of the learned'. On succeeding to the throne in AD 813, Al-Mamun applied himself vigorously to the advancement of learning – founding universities, funding scholars and translators, ordering the creation of terrestrial and celestial maps.

It was almost inevitable that the Great Pyramid should now become the object of renewed attention, especially since one of the legends asserted that it contained a secret chamber crammed with maps of the heavens and earth. (In various forms, this legend continues to thrive in the twenty-first century.) In the year 820, so the Arab chronicles say, Al-Mamun travelled to Giza with an entourage of stonemasons, engineers and architects, searching for the entrance. If it was still concealed by Strabo's hinged door, that door must have been a superb piece of work, for Al-Mamun's team soon gave up, baffled.

Turning to more direct methods, he ordered his men to gouge their way into the stone by brute force. No luck: the masonry was too solid for the small hammers and chisels they had brought along. So they resorted to an even blunter method of excavation. Giant fires were started on the surface of the rock, heating it until it was red-hot: then cold vinegar was poured on to the glowing stones until they cracked. Finally, a battering ram smashed aside the debris.

It was crude, but effective. Al-Mamun's men then tunnelled their way the better part of 100 feet (30 metres) inside the Pyramid – a task which became more unpleasant and more dangerous the deeper they went, choking on dust, gasping in the air that became more and more poisoned by their candles and their breath. Up to this point, the details of Al-Mamun's enterprise are reasonably well established, though not entirely uncontested – one source states that the Pyramid was already long since opened when his men arrived. Another suggests that all the team did was to widen a tunnel that had been dug by robbers in the ancient past. At any rate, the tunnel is there for all to see – ten courses too low, too far to the west, but still intact and now used as the tourist entrance.

From this point on, the story of Al-Mamun's excavation becomes more a matter of charming myth than of sober history. Here is one of the more colourful versions, derived from a historian with the splendidly sonorous name of Abu Abd Allah Mohammed ben Abdurakin Alkaisi.

The diggers were on the point of giving up when the noise of a dislodged rock, somewhere to their east, drew their attention. They changed direction, dug towards it, and eventually met the descending passage – 'exceedingly dark, dreadful to look at, and difficult to pass'. On the floor was a stone which had been dislodged from the ceiling by their digging. They clambered up the passage and found the real secret entrance; they crawled back down and found the nasty pit described by Strabo.

Returning to that fallen stone, they saw, through the hole it left in the ceiling, the edge of a rectangular red granite plug – a detail not mentioned by Strabo or any other classical source. They tried to chip it away, but found that it was not only too hard but also jammed in place by the weight of many tons. Had they stumbled across hidden treasure? They began to cut their way, not through the granite, but around it, scrabbling away the softer limestone. Six feet (2 metres) behind the plug was another, equally tightly wedged; behind that, another; behind that, another ....

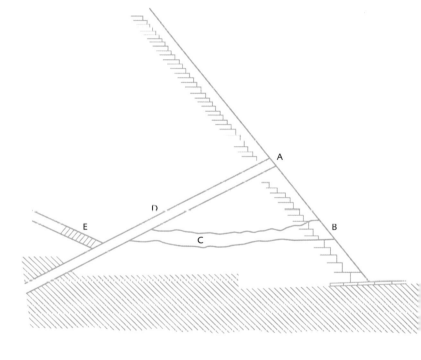

Section showing Al-Mamun's breach.

KEY

A Original entrance

B Al-Mamun's entrance

C Al-Mamun's forced passage

D Descending passage

E Granite plug

Eventually, more than twenty plugs later, they found softer rock. Tunnelling more quickly, they suddenly came upon a narrow ascending passage. This they climbed, until it gave out and they met with two tantalizing sights: above them, a black void; ahead, a low horizontal passage. And at the end of this was a large, bare room, with an empty niche in one wall and a gabled ceiling. Because the Arabs built gabled tombs for women and flat ones for men, they decided that this must be the Queen's Chamber. They were also tempted by the notion that the niche might give on to a second chamber, but gave up after hacking a yard or so into the masonry.

Going back to the ascending passage, they then tried to see what might be above them, waving their torches as high as they would go. They noticed that there were joist-holes in the side walls, and guessed, rightly, that the floor of the ascending chamber had once risen uninterruptedly, sealing off the passage to the Queen's Chamber. By climbing on each other's shoulders, the men were finally able to see that they were now at the bottom of a narrow but imposing gallery, rising off into the void.

The centre of this gallery was slippery, but at the side were ramps which offered footholds. They clambered up the ramps, torches held high, for a further 120 feet (36 metres), until they came to a large stone platform. This platform led into an antechamber ... and the rest of the story will by now be obvious. The King's Chamber was empty except for an abandoned sarcophagus. (A still more fanciful account contradicts this, claiming that the sarcophagus contained the statue of a man, with a glowing ruby on his head and armour of jewel-encrusted gold across his breast.) Bitterly disappointed, the Arabs hacked at the empty walls in a blind rage; to pacify them, some said, Al-Mamun had his servants 'plant' some gold there for his men to discover. They retreated, and for the next three or four centuries the Pyramid went all but unvisited.

The tale undeniably has its romance, but it is hard to reconcile either with other historical sources or with common sense. If the King's Chamber had been stripped by raiders, why was the system of granite blocks so perfectly intact? If it had not been raided, why had the Pyramid's builders gone to such inordinate effort and danger to protect an empty tomb? But the story retains its value – even if it was not Al-Mamun who first discovered the Queen's and King's Chambers, a sequence of events similar in most details to this one outlined by the Arab chroniclers must have happened, probably (as Petrie estimated) some time in antiquity. The fact that the usually conscientious Strabo does not mention the ascending passage implies either that it had been successfully resealed long before his visit (and this is generally considered the more likely option) or that the first breach was made between the Roman and Arab periods.

LEGENDS AND LOOTERS

It would probably be fair to credit Al-Mamun with relatively lofty motives for tomb raiding – to use an anachronistic term, he approached the task in a scientific spirit. He was the last known figure to do so for a very long time. Arab folklore dressed up the Pyramid in dark and ominous terms. At noon and at sunset, the people said, it was haunted by a fanged, naked woman – a sort of daylight vampire who seduced men and drove them mad.

In the twelfth century a scholarly traveller from Navarre, Rabbi Benjamin ben Jonah, gazed at the structures of the Giza plateau and concluded that they must have been built by witchcraft. The historian Abd-al-Latif, writing in the thirteenth century, confessed that he was so overcome by superstitious dread when he

A looted tomb, as depicted in a Swedish journal in 1923 at the height of the Egyptian craze that followed the discovery of Tutankhamun's tomb the previous year.

entered its interior that he fainted and had to be dragged out. It was Abd-al-Latif who reported that the surface of the Pyramid was inscribed with so many unintelligible characters that they would have filled ten thousand pages; most readers have assumed that, unless this description was purely fanciful, he was referring to the accumulated graffiti of the ages rather than to carved hieroglyphs.

In the fourteenth century, a book of travels attributed to 'Sir John Mandeville' reports that he dared not enter the Great Pyramid because it swarmed with countless serpents; but as the whole book was a pack of amusing tall tales cobbled together by a notary from Liège, this is, again, either pure nonsense or the echo of a received idea. Probably the latter, since Mandeville also reported of the Giza pyramids that 'some men say that they be sepultures of great lords, that were sometime, but that is not true, for all the common rumour and speech is of the people there, both far and near, that they be the garners [granaries] of Joseph'.

This was such a commonly repeated tale that it found its way even into the accounts of travellers who appear to have witnessed the pyramids at first hand and would therefore have recognized the likely foolishness of this reading – a striking instance of the triumph of prejudice over perception. The widespread fallacy is also immortalized in a twelfth-century mosaic, visible to this day in one of the domes in St Mark's, Venice, which shows biblical workmen piling sheaves into the open sides of granaries. Presumably as a result of artistic stylization rather than ignorance of their actual proportions, the pyramids are shown as being only about twice the height of a man.

Not everyone, however, was put off by the stories of vampires and serpents, especially if they had heard legends of a different kind which spoke of treasures in vast quantities. It is said that by the fourteenth century grave-robbing was considered a perfectly respectable craft in Cairo, and the aspiring tomb raider could even buy guidebooks to assist him. Not all of them reached the highest standards of accuracy: the Arabic text known as *The Book of Buried Pearls* (full title: *... and of the precious Mystery, giving Indications regarding the Hiding Places of Finds and Treasures*) tells its gullible purchaser that on entering the Pyramid

> you will see, to right and left, many rooms and, before you, a large hall containing the body of one of the first kings of Egypt. This king is surrounded by other kings and by his son, all of them clothed in gowns embroidered with gold thread and decorated with precious stones. Close by them you will see piles of silver, rubies, fine pearls, and gold and silver statues and idols. In this great heap you must search for a recess, richly inlaid in wood and enclosing a grotto.
>
> In this grotto you will see a large monolith which you will be able to move to one side, and thereby reveal a well containing a great deal of silver deposited there by the pagans.
>
> Take as much of it as you wish.
>
> God is most wise.

In 1900, one conservator declared that this little book had destroyed more ancient monuments than all the Egyptian wars put together.

THE EUROPEANS RETURN

One major spur to the revival of European interest in the Great Pyramid was the Crusades in the eleventh and twelfth centuries. Soldiers returning from their periods of holy warfare liked to awe their stay-at-home compatriots with tales of the wonders they had witnessed in the East. Eventually, a more serious and far-reaching version of this renewed attention to all things eastern came to inspire a new type of thinker in Italy. Schoolchildren are usually told that the Renaissance sprang from a rediscovery of the achievements of Greece and Rome. True enough, but they are not so often informed that some of the makers of the Renaissance nursed an equally profound admiration for Egypt – generally regarded as the ultimate source of all wisdom and all the arts.

A crucial moment in this development came in 1460, when the Florentine statesman and patron of the arts Cosimo de' Medici ordered the great scholar-philosopher Marsilio Ficino to translate the *Corpus Hermeticum* of Hermes Trismegistus, 'Thrice-Great Hermes', insisting that this task take priority even over work on something as crucial to Western civilization as Plato's *Republic*. The actual nature of this curious text has been fiercely disputed: some have claimed that is it indeed, as the Renaissance believed, of ancient Egyptian origin, dating to well before the fifth century BC; others that it post-dates Plato, and comes from the third century BC; others still that it is as recent as the second or third century AD. (Flinders Petrie held that at least some parts of the work must date back to the fourth century BC, although his claim provoked howls of rage among scholars.) The most satisfactory account may be that this is a mongrel collection of texts, written at various times from the sixth century BC to the second century AD.

Whatever its date, two points are clear. The first is that the 'Hermes Trismegistus' supposed to have written these works was traditionally identified with the Egyptian god of wisdom, Thoth, one of the most important deities in the ancient pantheon, and the object of a major cult which thrived particularly in the Ptolemaic period. (At various other periods of antiquity Thoth was demoted from god to sage, assumed by the Egyptians to be an actual historical figure and credited with the invention of writing, astronomy and numbers.) The second is that many Renaissance thinkers believed it to be the Key of Keys into lost wisdom.

Under the influence of Ficino's work, and of later contributions by the mystic writer Pico della Mirandola, Italy, and then the rest of Europe, relearned a respect for ancient Egypt that bordered on awe. From the fifteenth to the seventeenth centuries, it is said, more Europeans were interested in travel to Egypt than to Greece. One reliable estimate, in the historian Serge Sauneron's *Collection des voyageurs orientaux en Egypte* (1970), states that more than 250 descriptions of the country were published between 1400 and 1700. It could be a hazardous pursuit. In 1581, the French traveller Jean Palerme went to the Great Pyramid and recalled that 'One gentleman eager to make the ascent did in fact reach the summit, but ... succumbed to vertigo, fell and was smashed to pieces. The crushed remains no longer looked like a human being.'

In some cases, the fascination with Egypt was rendered more urgent by – again – the belief in lost wisdom, but in this case the quest was practical rather than esoteric. Although the age of the great explorations had prompted intense activity among astronomers and geographers, the state of those disciplines was still relatively crude. Could the ancient Egyptians be called on to lend a hand? Some thought they could: the Milanese scientist Girolamo Cardano, a good friend of Leonardo da Vinci, postulated that Egypt had possessed modes of calculation which had been preserved only imperfectly by the Greeks (Pythagoras himself, it was rumoured, had said something of the sort). It seemed plausible that the pyramids of Giza had been intended both to symbolize the precise dimensions of the earth and to set up an exact standard of measurement. Cardano's belief did not necessarily involve any assumption of mystical or occult knowledge on the part of the Egyptians – simply a superior ability in mathematics. Only in later generations did the really strange claims begin.

For all this intense and various interest, pyramid expeditions on anything like a serious scale did not begin until the seventeenth century. A traveller named Jean de Thevenot (1633–67) went to Egypt in 1652, made his way to Giza and executed reasonably accurate measurements of the Great Pyramid, both inside and out. Disappointingly, he appears to have been motivated as much by idle curiosity as by any more noble aim; yet, at about the same time he was busy with his notebook, a major intellectual figure back in Europe was already laying the earliest true foundation stones of a new intellectual discipline.

ATHANASIUS KIRCHER: THE FIRST EGYPTOLOGIST

The great Jesuit polymath Athanasius Kircher (1602–80) never went to Egypt, but is generally credited with being the earliest practitioner of Egyptology as a rigorous, or would-be rigorous, field of study. Sometimes derided by later commentators, his achievements in this sphere – as in the many others which his capacious mind addressed, from vulcanology and optics to music and magnetism – were actually very remarkable.

He became fascinated by Egypt as early as 1628, when he found a book illustrating hieroglyphics, regarded at the time as merely decorative. Kircher immediately grasped that this must be wrong, and set out on a lifelong quest to understand them. Scholars believe his greatest single work to be the *Oedipus Ægyptiacus* (1652–4), the frontispiece of which shows an implausibly young, athletic and heroic-looking Kircher, in knee-length robes, addressing a tiny and rather cute Sphinx. Kircher surmised, rightly, that there must be some link between the Coptic language and that of pharaonic Egypt, but failed to follow through this brilliant insight because he was committed to a symbolic rather than a linguistic reading of hieroglyphs. He has been mocked for this obsession, but, unlike Champollion who eventually 'cracked the code' (see pages 137–40), he possessed few clues to hint at the error of his approach – certainly no Rosetta

Portrait of Kircher in 1664 aged sixty-two.

Stone. His 'translations' of hieroglyphic inscriptions were made in good faith, but can only be accounted fanciful.

Kircher went on to publish two more Egyptological works, *Obeliscus Ægypticanus* (1666) and *Sphinx Mystagoga* (1676), the latter inspired by some mummy cases that had recently been brought to Europe. But it was in his last great work, *Turris Babel* (1679), that he most fully addressed the Pyramid itself. The illustration, drawn to his own exact specifications, is in some respects quaint (it shows the Sphinx as a giant bust of a woman, in the Greek style) and in others misleading (it shows ground-level entrances on two of the Pyramid's faces, as well as stairwells leading down to crypts). None the less, his work conveys both the amazing scale of the building and the basic nature of its inner structure.

Kircher derived his understanding of the Pyramid from an account written by the aristocratic traveller Prince Radziwill, and attributed its building to 'Chemis' – a Greek form of 'Cheops', which he considered synonymous with 'Cham', or Ham, the rebellious son of Noah. (Incidentally, Kircher worked out that the Flood had taken place in 2396 BC, 1567 years after the Creation. Coincidentally, 2396 is not too bad a guess for the actual date of the Pyramid.) After the waters of the Flood had receded, it was Ham's task to colonize Egypt; and the devout Kircher laid the blame for all subsequent religious 'error' on Ham and his descendants, 'from whom like a Trojan Horse came all the antique philosophies of the eternity and plurality of worlds, the life and divinity of the stars, the absurd dogmata of metempsychosis and the transmigration of souls, opening the window to all impiety'.

Above left Frontispiece of Kircher's *Oedipus Ægyptiacus* (1652–4).

Above right Illustration of the Great Pyramid from Kircher's *Turris Dabel* (1679).

The religion of ancient Egypt, Kircher felt, was the source of all subsequent false paths in spirituality, from the pantheistic beliefs of Greece and Rome to the 'pagan' faiths of India, China, Japan and the Americas. From this point of view, the Great Pyramid plainly had immense significance. Kircher also thought that the pyramidal shape of buildings found everywhere from China to South America (he had read Cortés's description of the Mexican pyramids) was yet further evidence that Egyptian religion and religious architecture had been diffused across the entire non-Christian world.

It was regrettable that Kircher, who recalled having travelled to other planets while in the grip of a musically induced trance, never went far from Rome in later life, for he was a sharp-eyed as well as a brilliant man, and might have contributed much more of lasting value to the discipline he had begun to establish. As it happened, the next great leap forward was made not by a Jesuit but by a Protestant.

JOHN GREAVES

In 1638, a young English mathematician and astronomer named John Greaves (1602–52) set off for Egypt on a momentous quest. Like Al-Mamun before him, he hoped that he might find in the Great Pyramid clues to the dimensions of the earth, in particular its circumference. With no less a luminary than the Archbishop of Canterbury as his patron (the clergyman wanted him to pick up some rare Arabic manuscripts on the way), Greaves bought measuring equipment (including a fine 10-foot (3-metre) measuring rod, skilfully divided into ten thousand units) and supplies. His first aim was to establish the ancient unit of measurement known to the Pyramid's builders – was it, for example, the Roman foot, the palm, the pace or perhaps the cubit?

After arriving at the Great Pyramid, Greaves scaled a mound of rubbish some 38 feet (12 metres) high and lowered himself, full of trepidation, into the descending passage. Almost at once he found himself in a blizzard of bats, 'so ugly and so large, exceeding a foot in length'. But he was a brave man as well as a good scholar and pressed on, retracing the path of previous explorers to the ascending passage, the Queen's Chamber (which stank so badly of vermin that he dared not enter), the Grand Gallery and the King's Chamber. Here, he deployed his measuring rod and set about recording the exact dimensions of everything he could find. Escaping from this foul interior, he then set about

Top Title page from John Greaves's *Pyramidographia* (London, 1646).

Above John Greaves, who measured the Giza pyramids with unprecedented accuracy in 1638.

surveying the exterior with equal care, and for the most part made an excellent job of it, estimating the original height to within a dozen feet (some 4 metres) of the correct figure.

Greaves is also the first man on record to have noted the existence of the narrow shaft which runs from the bottom of the Grand Gallery and all the way down to the bottom of the descending passage. The air here was so foul, and so thick with bats, that he decided (probably wisely) against trying to make a descent; but he did drop a lighted flare into its murk, and saw that light continue to flicker faintly even when he had lost track of the flare itself.

Before he left Egypt for good he donated his measuring equipment to a young Venetian gentleman, Tito Livio Burattini, who had been dispatched to the pyramids by Kircher. Burattini spent the next four years in Egypt, measuring and filing reports back to Kircher in Rome.

Meanwhile, John Greaves had returned to England, been appointed Savilian Professor of Astronomy at Oxford, written up his results and published them in 1646 as *Pyramidographia: Or, a Description of the Pyramids in Ægypt*. As a piece of sober historical investigation, it was admirable. Dismissing all suggestions that the Giza pyramids were the work of figures from the Bible or legend, he returned to the more reliable classical sources and identified them as the work of Cheops (Khufu), Chephren (Khafre) and Mycerinus (Menkaure); he also concluded that they were places built to enclose and protect royal bodies, in the belief that this would also guarantee the endurance of the soul.

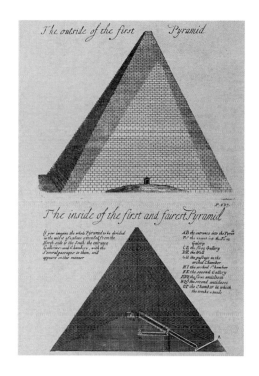

John Greaves's *Pyramidographia* included the first measured cross-section of the Great Pyramid.

As a survey, it was almost equally admirable. Apart from the unprecedented accuracy of his measurements, Greaves was sharp-eyed enough to notice the basalt pavement to the east of the Great Pyramid and learned enough to identify it as a possible mortuary temple. Interestingly, he also describes Khafre's pyramid as being smoothly encased except on the south side; today, only the casing on the upper third has been left intact. For all his talent, courage and industry, however, his results were flawed. The base of the Pyramid was so badly littered with rubble that he underestimated its length by a good 70 feet (21 metres), a degree of error large enough to throw his calculations out completely.

Unaware of these limitations, Sir Isaac Newton seized on Greaves's figures and used them to deduce that the Pyramid had been built on the basis of two

Sir Isaac Newton (1642–1727) in a portrait by Sir Godfrey Kneller, 1702 (detail).

distinct units of measurement, the 'profane' (or 'Memphis') cubit, about 21 inches (53 cm) long, and the 'sacred' cubit, about 25 inches (63 cm) long. His study bore the unwieldy title: *A Dissertation upon the Sacred Cubit of the Jews and the Cubits of several Nations: in which from the dimensions of the Greatest Pyramid as taken by Mr. John Greaves, the ancient Cubit of Memphis is determined.*

Few readers of this tract would have been aware of its greater significance in Newton's intellectual career: his general theory of gravitation, not yet announced, depended on an accurate knowledge of the earth's circumference. If Newton could find the precise length of the cubit, he could then work out the Egyptian *stadium*, said by classical sources to be directly in proportion to one geographical degree. Newton's calculations, it almost goes without saying, were brilliant; but Greaves's data were flawed, and his work therefore in vain. Newton left the gravitational work unpublished for several more years, until others – the man who usually gets the credit is Jean Picard, although others had anticipated him – had worked out the length of a degree by astronomical and geometrical rather than archaeological means.

Interest in the Great Pyramid, and in the still infant science of Egyptology, continued to increase steadily throughout the late seventeenth and eighteenth centuries. As one Parisian writer noted in 1740: 'The only things talked about are the ancient cities of Thebes and Memphis, the Libyan Desert, and the caves of the Thebaid. The Nile is as familiar to many people as the Seine. Even the children have their ears battered with its cataracts and openings.'

OTHER EIGHTEENTH-CENTURY EGYPTOMANES

However much Egyptomania might rage in northern Europe, the harsh realities of travel in the country itself put something of a damper on all but the most courageous or reckless. Nominally governed by the Ottoman Turks, much of Egypt teemed with bandits and was hazardous in the extreme. Nevertheless, during this period leading up to Napoleon's campaign there were still some who explored and described the Great Pyramid.

Benoit de Maillet, French consul-general in Egypt from 1692 to 1708, was a forerunner of all those nineteenth-century politicians, functionaries and bureaucrats who went on a more or less licensed orgy of antiquity-looting for the benefit of European collectors and museums. He visited Khufu's Pyramid about forty times, and in his *Description of Egypt*, published in 1735, provided not only the fullest account of the entire country since the Roman occupation, but an extremely accurate estimate of the Great Pyramid's dimensions, as well as the first cross-section diagram. He erred mainly in making the structure too tall and narrow.

Following in the footsteps of Kircher, another Jesuit, Father Claude Sicard (1677–1726), visited and investigated some twenty pyramids and other ancient monuments between 1707 and 1726. He is credited with producing in 1717 the first modern map of Egypt, a watercolour detailing all the major sites between Aswan in the south and the Mediterranean in the north. Father Sicard died of plague at the age of fifty, having just completed a work comparing the geographies of ancient and modern Egypt.

Nathaniel Davison, later to be British consul-general in Algeria, can be credited with discovering a major secret of the Pyramid's inner structure — perhaps even two secrets. First, he was daring enough to attempt the task that Greaves had forgivably shirked, and, with a rope tied round his waist, had himself lowered down the shaft that runs vertically from the Grand Gallery. After about 200 feet (60 metres) or so he came to rest on sand and rubble – rather an anticlimactic reward for his bravery. This debris, which blocked the connection between the shaft and the descending passage, was not removed for another half-century.

Davison met with much more thrilling results higher up in the Pyramid. Noticing that his voice echoed from high above him in a curious way when he shouted in the Grand Gallery, and assuming that the shape of the Gallery itself was not causing this effect, he set about searching for another cause. Waving about a candle fixed at the end of a long pole, he finally spotted a very small hole, barely 2 feet (60 cm) wide, at the highest point where the Gallery's wall met its ceiling.

Using a set of seven short ladders, Davison made the extremely hazardous ascent of the Gallery's slippery walls. Had he fallen, he would almost certainly have been killed. On 8 July 1765 he reached the hole, only to find it almost entirely blocked by 16 inches (40 cm) of accumulated bat dung, as pungent as it was thick. Not daunted, he tied a handkerchief over his mouth and nose, forced his way through the smelly mass and squirmed his way 25 feet (7.6 metres) along a narrow passage until it opened up into a shallow room, not high enough to stand up in but otherwise with exactly the same dimensions as the King's Chamber below. He had discovered the first and lowest of the hollow rooms that protect the King's Chamber from the mass of masonry above it. His courage won him a small measure of immortality: this space has been known ever since as Davison's Chamber.

A couple of other pre-Napoleonic travellers are worthy of brief mention. The English antiquarian Richard Pococke and his Danish counterpart Frederik Norden both visited in 1737. Pococke advanced the view that the Pyramid had been made by building a giant case around a huge mound of solid rock. Norden, who had trained as a marine architect, produced the most accurate measurements of the Pyramid to date.

THE CONNECTION WITH FREEMASONRY

As the eighteenth century drew to a close, the imminent explosion of Egyptological studies was gathering momentum. One last, curious episode in this story should be noted before moving on, however, and that is the rise of Freemasonry as a political and cultural force. Although the story is clouded by cranks and obsessives, a few details are beyond dispute. Whatever its precise origins, Freemasonry undeniably played an extremely significant role in the eighteenth-century scientific, political and cultural advances which we now call the Enlightenment, and in the social and nationalistic upheavals which are a major dimension of that Enlightenment. Most of the major figures of the Enlightenment were either masons or influenced by Freemasonry; and the masons were all Egyptophiles, in some cases claiming that they drew their traditions from secret Egyptian texts, in other cases actually asserting an unbroken lineage back to Egyptian priesthoods.

The masons saw their lodges as Egyptian temples and decorated them with all manner of Egyptian symbols, including the still misunderstood hieroglyphs: hence, among other phenomena, the image of the pyramid and the eye, placed on the reverse of the Great Seal of the United States of America and reproduced on the dollar bill. And although it remains uncertain whether Napoleon himself was a mason, it is a matter of record rather than conspiratorial theory that he was involved in certain masonic affairs, that some of his imperial emblems were masonic-Egyptian, and that Freemasonry flourished under his rule.

The time was ripe for the theory of Egyptophilia to be carried into practice on a massive scale.

Top Pyramid imagery on a French masonic apron of the early nineteenth century.

Above The reverse side of the Great Seal of the United States of America, with its all-seeing 'third eye' of Horus. The Latin inscriptions read *Annuit Cœptis* ('has looked with favour on the beginnings') and *Novus Ordo Seclorum* ('a new order of ages').

CHAPTER SEVEN

THE ORIGINS OF MODERN EGYPTOLOGY

NAPOLEON'S INVASION OF EGYPT

THE MOST IMPORTANT DATE in the modern history of the Great Pyramid is 19 May 1798, the day on which Napoleon sailed from the southern French port of Toulon to launch his invasion of Egypt. The general, just twenty-nine years old, was in charge of a fleet of 328 vessels – barely adequate to contain his army of thirty-five thousand. His primary objectives were, of course, political and military. At the very least, by overthrowing the ruling Mameluke powers – the Ottoman Turkish warrior class – and occupying the country he would be able to block the most significant of the trade routes between Britain and India. But he was also tantalized by the prospect of a further push east and the capture of India itself; and haunted by the precedent of Alexander the Great, who had failed in the same ambition.

Above **Napoleon Bonaparte. Detail from a painting by Antoine-Jean Gros, 1797.**

Previous page
The Battle of the Pyramids in a painting by François Watteau.

After disembarkation at Alexandria, Napoleon's armies marched across the desert with Cairo in their sights. Meanwhile, the Mameluke leader Murad Bey assembled a force of ten thousand horsemen to repel the invader. The opposing forces met on 12 July at Imbaba, west of Cairo, within sight of the Giza plateau. According to legend, Napoleon exhorted his troops by shouting: 'Soldiers, from the heights of these pyramids forty centuries are watching you!' (At any rate, the phrase was later inscribed on a commemorative medal.) Whether or not this is true, the result – now known as the Battle of the Pyramids – was a massacre. A force of the kind which had once withstood Genghis Khan was powerless against modern cannon and sharpshooters. Within barely two hours, two thousand Mamelukes lay dead or dying; the French death toll was reckoned at little more than forty. Murad's men scattered and dispersed into Upper Egypt, where one of Napoleon's generals pursued and harassed them for many months. Cairo fell to the French with no further struggle, and Napoleon was master of Egypt.

But the British were about to strike back. In August the Royal Navy, under Nelson, attacked and destroyed the French fleet at Abukir Bay. For the next three years, until their eventual rout in 1801, the French were virtual prisoners of their own conquest. That interval of three years revolutionized the study of ancient Egypt.

Napoleon's hand written notes on his own sketch of the Giza pyramids.

THE WORK OF NAPOLEON'S *SAVANTS*

In addition to his soldiers, Napoleon had brought to Egypt 175 highly erudite men: his *savants*. During the enforced leisure of their Egyptian sojourn these men, organized into a Commission on Arts and Sciences, set about mapping, collecting, digging and drawing every aspect of the country from its birds and animals to its irrigation systems. Naturally, the Great Pyramid was a major focus of investigation.

The most important contributions to the Giza survey were made by four men. An architect, J. M. Lepère, joined one of Napoleon's staff, Colonel Jean-Marie Joseph Coutelle, in making a careful survey of the interior structure, while Edmé-François Jomard, a surveyor, and an artist-engineer named Cécile addressed themselves to its overall dimensions. In 1801, Lepère and Coutelle also began to take apart the westernmost of the three queens' pyramids.

Each of these men left anecdotal as well as scientific accounts of their ventures. Coutelle, for example, recorded the unpleasant experience of being attacked by clouds of angry bats, 'who scratched with their claws and stifled with the acrid stench of their bodies', while Jomard recalled climbing all the way to the top of the Pyramid and then trying to throw a stone beyond its base, using a slingshot. He failed. But, with the help of 150 Turkish labourers, he was able to clear the northeast and northwest corners of the Pyramid of its layers of debris, uncover the site of the original cornerstones, and thus measure the base length of the Pyramid more exactly than any previous explorer.

It was a matter of more than purely antiquarian interest for Jomard. He was in passionate search of confirmation that the ancient Egyptians had indeed, as legend claimed, known the exact circumference of the earth, and that the Pyramid's dimensions encoded both this figure and specific indications of latitude. Sure enough, Jomard found all the confirmation he was looking for, both geological and geographical, as well as some surprises. Napoleon's surveyors had discovered that if they used the apex of the Pyramid to establish a north–south meridian line, that line would neatly separate the Nile delta area into two equal portions; furthermore, that two diagonal lines drawn through the Pyramid's edges to the northwest and northeast would enclose the delta with equal neatness. Other, less sober writers have made much of this, as we shall see in Chapter 9.

One of the curiosities of Jomard's career was that he held on to his findings for the better part of three decades, and when he finally published them in two books of 1829 – *Description générale de Memphis et ses pyramides*, and *Remarques et recherches sur les pyramides d'Egypte* – the fickle intellectual classes of Europe had already started to grow a little bored with Egypt and were now well in the middle of a revived Hellenophile craze: once again Greece was idolized, Egypt scorned, and most people who read the astonishing correspondences noted by Jomard assumed that he was either mistaken or a fraud.

By the time Napoleon was halfway through his enforced Egyptian sojourn, he too had become fascinated by some of the more arcane aspects of the Pyramid. On 12 August 1799 (or 25 Thermidor, according to the French Revolutionary calendar), he visited Giza with Imam Muhammed as his guide, and asked to be left alone for a while in the King's Chamber. Once again he had the precedent of Alexander the Great in mind, for the earlier conqueror of Egypt was said to have done just this. On emerging from the Chamber Napoleon seemed shaken, and was angry with his lieutenants when they jokingly asked him if he had seen anything strange. He never spoke directly about the experience, although many years later, when a prisoner on St Helena, he seemed about to confess, only to break off, saying, 'No, what's the use? You'd never believe me.'

After the French had returned home – the victorious British granted safe passage to the *savants* whom Napoleon had abandoned there, treating them as civilians – the Egyptological work began in earnest. Napoleon commissioned an epic work summarizing the *savants*' findings, with the appropriately protracted title *Description de L'Egypte, ou Recueil des observations et des recherches qui ont*

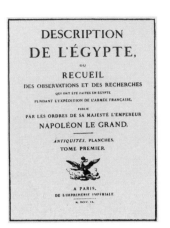

Title page from the epic
Description de L'Egypte.

été faites en Egypte pendant l'expédition de l'armée française. It was published over the course of thirteen years, and everything about the project was on a grand scale: nine folio volumes of text, eleven volumes of plates, three thousand illustrations by two hundred artists ... the finished product was so large that it came with a specially designed wooden cabinet.

EGYPYTOMANIA GRIPS THE FRENCH

But the *Description* had a good deal of its thunder stolen by a much smaller and far more modestly priced book, the *Voyage dans la Basse et la Haute Egypte* of 1802 by the Baron Dominique Vivant Denon (1747–1825), a colourful character even by the lively standards of Egyptology. A sometime pornographer, and notable wooer and flatterer of powerful women from Madame de Pompadour to Catherine II of Russia, Denon somehow managed to keep his head firmly clamped to his shoulders during the Terror; then, applying his charms to Josephine, he wangled a place in Napoleon's invasion fleet before taking off on researches of his own.

On his return to Paris, Denon was put in charge of France's museums and founded the Musée Napoleon – now the Louvre. Rapidly written, his *Voyage* was an even more rapid success, thanks in no small part to his skill as an illustrator. The book soon ran into no fewer than forty editions, with translations into English and German following swiftly on the French publica-

Baron Dominique Vivant Denon in a portrait by Robert Lefevre, 1808 (detail).

tion. Denon's book initiated a major fad. Egypt – already a fashionable interest for many decades – suddenly became the object of an unprecedented craze. When the first volumes of *Description* began to appear, Egyptomania reached epidemic proportions.

Some aspects of this craze were entirely harmless – the so-called 'Egyptian Revival' style, for one. No fashionable French household was now complete

without its chairs in the manner of mortuary furnishings, its sphinx-shaped ink-stands, its candelabra festooned with (still incomprehensible) hieroglyphics. Other aspects were baleful, above all the orgy of European looting – both by 'scholars' and by confessed fortune-hunters – which was now unleashed on the country, and which made the scale of all previous looting seem like petty larceny.

EGYPTIAN LOOT FOR EUROPEAN KNOW-HOW

One of those who must take their share of the blame is Mohammed Ali (1769–1849), appointed Turkish viceroy of Egypt in 1805, who not merely tolerated this large-scale plunder but even encouraged it. In principle, he was answerable to the Sultan in Constantinople; in practice, he was a new pharaoh. From about 1810 to 1850, under Ali's *laissez-faire* regime, everyone from small-time crooks to grand diplomats enjoyed an open season on antiquities. (This is not the only stain on Mohammed Ali's reputation. In 1811 he arranged a massacre, in the citadel of Cairo, of all those Mamelukes who contested his rule.)

Ali's ambition was the modernization of his country, and in order to establish the industrial base needed by all modern nations he called in a flock of specialists, often doubtfully qualified, from all over Europe. A rough system of reciprocal favours came into play at government level. In return for helping him out with the import of machinery and other essential supplies from Europe, Ali would grant foreign consuls a *firman* – a document authorizing the recruitment of local manpower. This was a cheap commodity if Ali approved, almost impossible to obtain if he refused. It was this bartering which led to the so-called 'war of the consuls', involving men such as Bernardino Drovetti, Jean-François Mimaut and Raymond Sabatier from France and Henry Salt from Britain.

Salt and Drovetti were particularly fierce sparring partners. The Italian-born Drovetti (1776–1852) had served under Napoleon during the Egyptian invasion, and in reward for his gallantry – he saved the life of Napoleon's future brother-in-law – was launched on a career in diplomacy. He was appointed French vice-consul in 1803, and consul-general in 1810. Briefly out of favour when Louis XVIII came to the throne in 1814, he bided his time as a freelance trader in antiquities until another change in the political wind brought him back to office from 1820 to 1829.

Drovetti's men scoured Egypt with insatiable greed. In the course of his career, he assembled and sold three gigantic collections. The first, bought by the King of Sardinia in 1824 and sent to the museum in Turin, contained more than a thousand artefacts, many of them magnificent. The second was bought by Charles X, King of France from 1824 to 1830, and formed the basis of the Egyptological collection at the Louvre. The third, smaller but no less remarkable, was sold to the King of Prussia.

Drovetti's English competitor Henry Salt, meanwhile, was every bit as busy. A trained artist, he was appointed consul in Egypt in 1816, and immediately set to work collecting. By 1818 he had built up his first major collection, and sold it – for a paltry £2000 – to the grudging Trustees of the British Museum, who proved not merely stingy but unperceptive: they turned down his best find, the alabaster sarcophagus of Seti I, which went instead to a private collector, the extraordinary Romantic architect and antiquarian Sir John Soane. Understandably miffed by his dealings with the British

Mohammed Ali, shown here in a coloured engraving of 1830, was Turkish viceroy of Egypt from 1805 until his death in 1849 and authorized the plundering of many of the country's ancient artefacts.

Museum, whose payment had not even covered the costs of excavation, Salt now put wallet before country and sold his next collection to Charles X in 1824 for the much more satisfactory figure of £10,000.

It is in the context of this trade war – a figurative conflict which sometimes resembled the actual thing, especially when Salt's men joined in running fights with Drovetti's – that yet another remarkable Italian comes on the scene. Salt's main agent was one Giovanni Battista Belzoni (1778–1823): a huge man, 6 feet 6 inches (2 metres) tall and heavily muscled, he had been by turns a student of hydraulics, a circus strongman (one of his stunts was the 'Human Pyramid'), an independent traveller and perhaps even a novice monk. He came to Egypt in 1814 with his Irish wife in the hope of working for Mohammed Ali, and devoted the better part of two years and all his savings to developing a superior form of water-wheel that might help revolutionize Egyptian agriculture. He had enemies in Ali's court, however, and although his invention was a technical triumph it was not adopted. Belzoni was left high and dry. A resourceful man, he then made contact with Salt and offered to secure him the massive head of Ramesses which had been uncovered at Thebes.

It was a daunting task, but, armed with a *firman*, Belzoni pulled it off in great style, turning each fresh obstacle (and there were many) into a fresh display of ingenuity and resourcefulness. But this was only the beginning of his feats as an explorer and excavator. He made one of the earliest investigations of the Great Temple of Abu Simbel, which had only been rediscovered as recently as 1813; he located the tomb of Seti I in the Valley of the Kings; and, of course, he re-explored the Great Pyramid and other Giza monuments.

By this stage of the game, a race was on between the forces aligned with France and those working with Britain. Drovetti, it was rumoured, was about to blast the Great Pyramid wide open using dynamite, but in the end Britain's Italian beat France's Italian. (Intrepid to a fault, Belzoni at one point managed to wedge himself so firmly into one of the Great Pyramid's narrower passages that his men had to yank him out.) His great coup was first to locate and then to open the long-lost entrance to the Great Pyramid's smaller sibling, Khafre's pyramid.

When his men had finally cleared away the rubble blocking his path, he found that he could make his way up the ascending passage, through the horizontal

Top Henry Salt in a portrait by John James Halls, 1815.

Above Giovanni Belzoni in Turkish dress.

passage and finally – after spending the better part of a month at the whole task – raise the granite portcullis to enter Khafre's burial chamber. Alas, the sarcophagus was empty, its granite lid cast to one side and broken in two. Graffiti on the wall in Arabic gave away the identity of the earlier tomb raiders – men, it is now estimated, of the thirteenth century AD. Belzoni also started exploring the third Giza pyramid, Menkaure's, but a major falling-out with Salt brought this venture to a premature end.

Henry Salt was a professional artist before he became the British consul-general in Egypt. This 1809 engraving by Daniel Havell is based on Salt's painting, *Pyramids at Cairo*.

DECODING THE HIEROGLYPHS

Although the story of how the ancient language of Egypt once again became intelligible does not immediately concern Khufu's monument, some mention should be made of the brilliant linguist Jean-François Champollion. Born in 1790, Champollion was a precocious if wilful student, at the age of thirteen refusing to have anything to do with arithmetic but cramming himself with the grammars and vocabularies of Arabic, Hebrew, Syriac and Chaldean (Aramaic) as well as the compulsory Greek and Latin.

Already the seeds of his ambition were ripening, and directed to one supreme end: understanding Egyptian. At the age of seventeen he learned Persian and Coptic, convinced that in Coptic he was seeing the ancient Egyptian language refracted through the medium of Greek. By eighteen he had his doctorate; by nineteen, he was a professor of ancient history at the University of Grenoble. But his rapid ascent of the ladder to fame was interrupted by politics, when Grenoble rallied to Napoleon's cause after he escaped from imprisonment on Elba in 1815. It was Champollion who was credited with climbing the local citadel and tearing down the white flag of the Bourbon king, Louis XVIII, who had replaced the Emperor as ruler of France. When Napoleon was defeated that year at Waterloo, Champollion was summarily dismissed and forced to support himself by opening a private school. Eventually he went to Paris, where he was finally able to gain access to some of the documents which would help him in his great ambition.

By now, the race to crack the hieroglyphic code was becoming fierce. Champollion's chief rival was an Englishman, Thomas Young (1773–1829), who was even more of a linguistic prodigy: at fourteen, Young not only knew all the languages Champollion had so far learned but had also mastered Italian, Turkish, even Ethiopian. More amazing still, Young was even more gifted as a natural scientist than as a linguist: he trained in medicine and botany, and was to make some major discoveries in physics. It was, perhaps, this exceptional range of interests which distracted him from single-minded attention to the Egyptian question.

All of the leading scholars racing to crack the code now had access to the single piece of evidence which would ultimately prove crucial: texts copied from the so-called Rosetta Stone – a fragment from a black basalt stele, uncovered near Alexandria by Napoleon's *savants* in 1799, surrendered to the British under the terms of the 1801 treaty, shipped to England and housed in the British Museum in 1802. The great promise offered by the Stone was that its three scripts – the top strip in hieroglyphics, the middle in a cursive script that looked similar to Arabic, and the bottom in Greek – gave every sign of being versions of the same text: a decree by Ptolemy V from around 196 BC. Champollion had first seen a plaster cast of the Stone when he was twelve: his life from that point on was a quest to understand it.

Although one should not underestimate the leap of imagination which enabled Champollion finally to crack the code, at the heart of his achievement was an insight that can be stated with extreme simplicity. Scholars had endlessly debated the question of whether the hieroglyphs were ideographic or phonetic:

Jean-François Champollion became a national hero in France when he used the Rosetta Stone to crack the hieroglyphic code in 1822. This promotional card from 1900 used his image to sell chocolate.

Opposite
The Rosetta Stone

that is, did the curious little pictures represent things (or ideas about things), or did they stand for sounds, much as the letters of an alphabet do? After a painstaking comparison of all the different inscriptions – the name 'Ptolemy' (or, more exactly, *ptolemaios*, its Greek form) was an important clue – Champollion suddenly realized the truth: Egyptian hieroglyphs were neither strictly phonetic, nor strictly ideographic, but *both*. Some of the symbols indicated sounds; another group of symbols – usually referred to nowadays as 'determinatives' – indicate to the reader what sort of phenomenon these sounds are indicating.

Champollion announced his findings in a letter sent to Monsieur Dacier of the French Académie des Inscriptions et Belles-Lettres on 27 September 1822.

Further researches soon confirmed that he was right; six years later Champollion realized his lifelong dream and travelled to Egypt, the first man for many centuries to be able to read the inscriptions that covered so many of the land's great monuments. He wrote up his results in *Monuments of Egypt and Nubia*, but the work was not published until 1845. By that time, Champollion had been dead for thirteen years.

Meanwhile, back in Egypt, activities around the Great Pyramid showed no sign of diminishing.

Howard Vyse (1784–1853) used dynamite to blast his way into the Great Pyramid in 1837.

COLONEL HOWARD VYSE

A former equerry to the Duke of Cumberland, a failed parliamentary candidate, an officer in Wellington's army (he was eventually promoted to the rank of general), a devout Christian, a petty tyrant, and a man rumoured to be almost wholly devoid of subtlety, humour or charm, Colonel Richard William Howard Vyse first encountered the pyramids of Giza on a moonlit ride on the opposite bank of the Nile in November 1836. He was entranced. It was the start of an obsession which led him to squander more than £10,000 of his inheritance on explorations, often employing as many as seven hundred local workers at a time. (Much taken with the theories of G. B. Caviglia about the Pyramid's mysterious origins, Vyse employed the Italian as superintendent of works until they fell out badly; more of this in Chapter 9.)

In 1837, he began a collaborative exploration of the Giza plateau with John Shea Perring (1813–69), an engineer. Based in the tombs to the east of the site, they organized a large local workforce which they drove as hard as Vyse typically drove himself. Vyse may not have had genius, but he had at his disposal a tool which no previous excavator had deployed: dynamite. At Khafre's pyramid, he used explosives to blast away the granite plugs which blocked its lower entrance.

Besides dynamite, Vyse also had the most modern drilling equipment, and used these tools with an abandon which would horrify modern archaeologists. He bored deep, for example, into one of the queens' pyramids by the pyramid of Menkaure; his vandalism was rewarded by the discovery of a young female skeleton in the burial chamber, and the name of Menkaure daubed in red on its ceiling. He also drilled deep into the back of the Sphinx until his rods would cut no deeper – they stopped at about 27 feet (8.2 metres) – and then set off explosions to try to free the rod. Few modern archaeologists can contemplate this action without shuddering.

Turning his attention to Menkaure's pyramid itself, he drilled a hole directly into its core, and then downwards towards the base, using repeated blasts of dynamite in the process. Although he found none of the new chambers for which he had hoped, he did

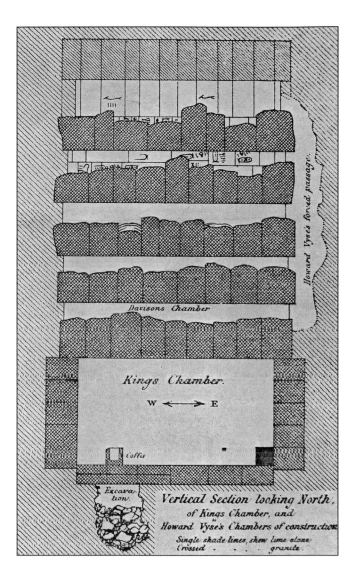

Cross-section (looking north) showing the construction of the stress-relieving chambers above the King's Burial Chamber and the passage blasted by Howard Vyse. Khufu's name was found painted in the uppermost chamber.

manage to locate the original entrance, clear it and make his way into the burial chamber with the artist Edward Andrews. Like Belzoni, they found Arabic graffiti which showed that the tomb had long since been looted, and once again the sarcophagus was all but empty.

The chamber did, however, contain human bones, the remnants of a coffin and an inscription identifying the room as Menkaure's resting place. (There were certain anomalies in these remains, which suggested that Menkaure's remains might have been reburied some two thousand years after he died; this is still a vexed, complex and slightly mysterious topic.) Vyse ordered his men to remove the lidless sarcophagus, which they duly did, with great effort, but subsequently the ship on which it was being taken to England sank in a Mediterranean storm.

Vyse decided to tackle the major landmark of the Giza site, Khufu's Pyramid, from the south side, using dynamite in an attempt to blast an entrance at about the same level as the northern entrance. He caused a great deal of pointless damage in the process, and gave up when it became evident that no new passage or set of passages were to be found there. Some small good came of this orgy of blasting, however: he did manage to uncover some of the white limestone casing blocks, as well as parts of the Pyramid's surrounding pavement.

But the discovery which really helps to justify Vyse's near-vandalizing of the monument – if anything can – took place well inside. He began to suspect that there might be another stress-relieving chamber immediately above Davison's Chamber, since he was able to insert a long, thin reed up into a crack which he found on that space's northeast roof. He called for his dynamite, and once again began to blast.

Over the next few months, Vyse gradually made his way up into all the remaining four empty chambers. He was the first man in over four thousand years to read all the red-paint graffiti, with its various construction notes, its names of work-gangs linked with the full royal name 'Khnum-khuf' and – in one place only – the simple name 'Khufu': overwhelming written proof that the Great Pyramid was indeed, as all the historians recorded, the tomb of the king known to the Greeks as Cheops. A keen patriot (and also, as cynics might say, a man who knew how to flatter his superiors), Vyse had no time for evocative, poetic or pseudo-Egyptian names for his discoveries, and simply christened each new chamber with the name of a British worthy: Wellington, after his former general; Nelson, after the admiral; Arbuthnot, as a homage to Lady Ann, wife of Sir Robert Arbuthnot, who had bestowed her gracious presence on the Pyramid excavations just after that chamber had been opened; and Campbell, after the British consul in Cairo, Colonel Campbell. On some diagrams, the chambers have kept these names to this day.

In 1840 Howard Vyse returned home, and published at his own expense *Operations Carried on at the Pyramids of Gizeh in 1837* – two handsome volumes which were graced with an unexpectedly learned anthology of writings by more than a hundred visitors from Herodotus onwards. A less happy aspect of the book, in the eyes of orthodox scholars, was the tremendous boost that its lists of measurements gave to the rapidly growing pseudo-science of 'pyramidology'.

THE SCHOLARS

In the four decades after Vyse's work and before that of Flinders Petrie the unbridled free-for-all of European looting at long last started to be regulated, and scholars began to put their researches on a more professional, less maverick basis. On the other hand, the pyramids ceased to be quite as exotic as they had once seemed, now that reasonably safe, comfortable travel in Egypt was becoming available to more and more people.

Three names dominate this period: those of Wilkinson, Lepsius and Mariette. (One of the other major figures of the day, Charles Piazzi Smyth, will be discussed later in the context of 'pyramidology', since his views were and still are held to be at best eccentric. For the time being, however, it is worth noting that some of the derision aimed at the Victorian astronomers and mathematicians who were 'seduced' by the formal elegance of the pyramids may have been due to their offence, not only against professional canons of acceptable scientific inquiry, but also against 'common sense' orthodox views on racial superiority and progress. To put it more bluntly, it was considered self-evident in many quarters that ancient people, above all those whose skin was not white, could not possibly have understood the intellectual complexities of higher geometry.)

The principal work of Sir John Gardner Wilkinson (1797–1875) was carried out in the area of Thebes quite early, from 1821 to 1833, but he lived so long that his influence remained strong for several decades afterwards and helped to put British Egyptology in much better order. His greatest work, *The Manners and Customs of the Ancient Egyptians* (1837), drew on many ancient texts and illustrations and was the pioneering inquiry into the daily lives and deaths of the lower classes in pharaonoic Egypt.

Karl Richard Lepsius (1810–84) was Wilkinson's counterpart in Germany. A scholar of classical archaeology and a formidable linguist, he had taught himself to read hieroglyphs from Champollion's posthumous works. Appointed lecturer in philology at Berlin, he was commissioned by the King of Prussia, Frederick William IV, to undertake a massive survey of Egypt and Nubia. Lepsius spent four years preparing for the task by scrutinizing every Egyptological collection in England, Italy and the Netherlands, and then, in 1842, set out with his team of scholars on a three-year expedition.

The fruit of their efforts was contained in Lepsius's *Discoveries in Egypt and Ethiopia*, which was published posthumously in twelve volumes between 1897 and 1913 and included no fewer than 894 large-scale illustrations. Although his

Top Sir John Gardner Wilkinson's notes and drawings are invaluable because they record ancient sites before they were damaged by tourists and subsequent, less scrupulous, archaeologists.

Above Karl Richard Lepsius undertook a three-year study of Egypt and Nubia from 1842.

Auguste Mariette, on the left in this photograph, supervising an excavation in Egypt towards the end of his life in 1878.

team's researches were wide-ranging and their observations say plenty about the country as a whole, Lepsius's principal contribution to the study of the pyramids was his so-called 'accretion theory'. This maintained that the size of any given pyramid was in direct proportion to the length of reign of the monarch who built it – the gigantic scale of Khufu's Pyramid would therefore indicate a very long reign, begun when Khufu was still young. Even though some pyramids seem to have undergone progressive enlargement in much the way Lepsius proposed, and Khufu was indeed young when he commanded the building of the Pyramid, the accretion theory is now usually considered mistaken.

After wincing through endless accounts of the plunder of Egypt either for gain or in the names of national prestige or learning, it is pleasant to turn to the career of Auguste Mariette (1821–81), the man who did more than anyone else to put an end to the looting and blasting, and to guarantee that at least some of Egypt's treasures stayed in Egypt. In 1858 plans were being drawn up, under the auspices of the French, for the building of the Suez Canal. The man in charge of the project, Ferdinand de Lesseps, persuaded Egypt's ruler of the day, Said Pasha, to give all surviving antiquities into the care of Mariette, who became the first Director of the Egyptian Antiquities Service – his local title being *Maamour*.

Up to this point, Mariette had been a humble and often painfully impoverished private scholar. At the age of twenty-one, working as a teacher in Boulogne, he had been asked to sort through a cache of papers left by his late cousin, Nestor L'Hôte. It was a fateful encounter. L'Hôte had been a draughtsman for Champollion, and when Mariette saw his fascinating drawings he was smitten. Later in life, joking about the hieroglyph which takes the form of a duck, Mariette observed that the Egyptian duck is a dangerous animal – one snap of its beak and you carry the germs of Egyptology all your life.

Before long, Mariette had given himself so thorough an amateur grounding in his new passion that he was able to amaze Champollion's successors at the Collège de France with the range of his learning. Heedless of his financial future, he threw in his secure teacher's post and moved to Paris, where he took a menial job at the Louvre and began to learn Coptic. By 1850, he was fluent enough to go to Egypt with the aim of buying Coptic manuscripts. But the monks with whom he was supposed to negotiate had recently been swindled by a couple of unscrupulous Englishmen, who had plied them with drink, so he failed in this mission. Ignoring this setback, he used his remaining funds to start excavating in Saqqara.

He soon proved to be an inspired archaeologist, and a very lucky one. On 27 October that year he discovered a sphinx, buried in the sand. Remembering an account of this site by Strabo, he realized with a thrill that he might have stumbled across a key marker towards the long-lost Serapeum of Memphis. On 1 December, he gathered his workforce together at sunrise and instructed them to dig along what he guessed to be the path of a buried avenue. The dig took longer than he expected, and drained his resources almost dry. By 11 February 1851, Mariette was both elated and desperate: he had finally reached the edge of the Memphis Serapeum, but was almost broke. Having previously worked privately and in secret, he was now forced to go public and appeal for funds. To his surprise, the French government eventually awarded him the more than generous sum of 30,000 francs.

Meanwhile, he had become world-famous in just a matter of months. Already, it was clear that Mariette was on to something big; by the time his excavations were completed he could be credited with one of the three or four greatest coups in the history of Egyptology – the unearthing of vast underground catacombs or burial chambers, eternal home to the mummified bodies of the sacred Apis bulls, each one encased in its own great sarcophagus made of a single granite block and beautifully polished to a mirror-like smoothness.

Mariette's appointment as Director of the new Egyptian Antiquities Service brought him both great freedom and great responsibility. On the one hand, he now had the funds, the manpower and the full official backing to go back and forth in Egypt as he saw fit, excavating and collecting at every major site. The new agreement stipulated that everything he collected would now be sent back to the capital and housed in the Cairo Museum, which he had just set up, in order to protect these valuable antiquities 'against the greed of the local peasants or the covetousness of Europeans'. And this is just what he did. But not even the energetic and resourceful Mariette could entirely curb so lucrative and ubiquitous a racket as the antiquities trade; and one unforeseen, unfortunate consequence of his actions was that it alerted many previously innocent locals to the market value of the objects that were literally lying all around them.

Still, his efforts were valuable and prodigious. He made further remarkable discoveries at Saqqara, which cast much light on the historical development of the pyramids. At Thebes, he found the mummy of the XVIIth Dynasty Queen Aahotep. At Giza, he unearthed the valley temple of Khafre's pyramid, where he found a statue now considered one of the greatest masterpieces of Egyptian art – a diorite figure of the king himself. And in the very last year of Mariette's life, one of his foremen managed to open the pyramid of Pepi I at Saqqara, so discovering the invaluable pyramid texts (see Chapter 4). It was all remarkable work, and Mariette deserves his measure of immortality; but it marks the end of Egyptology's early stage rather than the origins of its maturity, which only begins with the work of Petrie.

Before moving on to that phase, however, let us look at the birth of another phenomenon which reaches down to the present day: tourism.

THE TOURISTS

By the beginning of the nineteenth century the popularity of Giza as a destination for intrepid travellers had been steadily increasing for some seven hundred years; but those who went there had been looters or scholars or soldiers or visionaries, not idlers in search of an amusing diversion or an unusual holiday resort. All this was now changing, and changing rapidly. Fortunately for posterity, one of this new generation of idlers also happened to be the greatest Western writer to have visited the place since Herodotus – the French novelist Gustave Flaubert (1821–80).

Flaubert travelled to Egypt in 1849: an unpublished, virtually unknown author who was about to turn twenty-eight. Literary history remembers Flaubert as a master of the realist mode, and his first masterpiece, *Madame Bovary*, as the work which changed the way novels could be written. As a young man, however, Flaubert was anything but a tough-minded realist. He was still in the thrall of Romanticism, and loved to fantasize about an 'Orient' he had encountered only in the pages of the *Arabian Nights* and modern poets such as Byron.

One of Flaubert's grand themes was illusion and disillusion: and the contrast between his youthful fantasies about the Great Pyramid and the reality recorded in his travel diaries is itself a small, quiet comedy of innocence clashing with experience. Four years before setting off to Egypt, Flaubert had written a fanciful account of what it must be like to scale the Pyramid   an extraordinary, overblown effusion which ended: 'Look! Lend an ear, listen and look, O traveller! O thinker! And your thirst will be appeased, and all your life will have passed like a dream, for you will feel your soul go out towards the light and soar in the infinite ....' So much for the exotic dream. Now for the reality: 'One is irritated by the number of imbeciles' names written everywhere: on the top of the Great Pyramid there is a certain Buffard, 79 Rue Saint-Martin, wallpaper-manufacturer, in black letters; an English fan of Jenny Lind's has written her name; there is also a pear, representing [the former French king] Louis-Philippe ....'

Flaubert, irritated by the morons who felt compelled to carve their names on everything in sight; slithering in bats' dung and comparing the descending passage to a sewer; curtly saluting a party of Englishmen who are crawling in as he crawls out ... this Flaubert is not only a different man from the adolescent lost in reveries of the Mysterious East, but – although the thought would no doubt have dismayed him – a novel kind of visitor to Khufu's tomb. Travel is one of the oldest of all human pursuits, but tourism as we know it today – democratic, mass tourism – is a very recent thing; Flaubert was recording the first stirrings not only of modern tourism (and its inevitable tendency to destroy mystery, for example by leaving its full name, address and occupation as Monsieur Buffard did) but also of the equally modern snobbery which derides tourism.

Another visitor to the pyramids wrote even more biliously about the barbaric manners of the modern tourists – the 'smoking, tobacco-stinking gentlemen and a few ladies, from some vulgar steamer', who messed about and performed silly

Top Gustave Flaubert photographed in 1870.

Above Samuel Langhorne Clemens (Mark Twain) photographed in 1900.

'whirling dances over King Cheops' tombstone [*sic*] with ignorant cursing of his ancient name'. He noted, too, 'the painful thunder of the coffer [sarcophagus] being banged, to close upon breaking, with a big stone swung by their Arab helps'. Another favourite pastime among the more loutish visitors was to climb to the summit, dislodge stones, and send them crashing down to join the rest of the accumulated rubble at the Pyramid's base.

At least Flaubert could console himself that, as a prosperous young man, he was still an independent traveller. Before too long, the travel companies had realized how much money could be made by herding people around foreign parts in large groups. The package tour was born, and one of the next great writers to make the pilgrimage to Giza came as a member of the first-ever organized tour of the pyramids. The year was 1867; the writer was called Samuel Langhorne Clemens (1835–1910), although he had already begun to make quite a reputation for himself under the pseudonym 'Mark Twain'. He wrote a knock-about account of his pyramidal adventures in *The Innocents Abroad* (1875): 'A laborious walk in the flaming sun brought us to the foot of the great Pyramid of Cheops. It was a fairy vision no longer. It was a corrugated, unsightly mountain of stone. Each of its monstrous sides was a wide stairway which rose upward, step above step, narrowing as it went, till it tapered to a point far off in the air ....'

Twain complains fulsomely about the noisy mob of local touts, guides and self-appointed experts who besiege the tourists without mercy, loudly insisting that they have no interest in *backsheesh* until their victims are well up the side of the Pyramid, at which point the guides turn strangely quiet and menacing, pointing out how far the fall is and what a shame it would be if one of the Americans should accidentally slip. He groans about the sheer torture for unathletic souls of being made to scale blocks that are as high as a dinner table, and of the impossibility of conveying to the men who are shoving and dragging you towards the summit with unseemly haste that you have no desire to race anybody and that a slow ascent will do nicely: 'Who shall say it is not a lively, exhilarating, lacerating, muscle-straining, bone-wrenching and perfectly excruciating pastime, climbing the Pyramids?' He reaches the top at last, and tries to console himself with the reflection that, as pagans, his 'Mohammedan' guides will eventually have their come-uppance in the next life.

The era of Romance, plainly, was at an end. So, too was the age of inspired and sometimes reckless amateurism in excavation and scholarship. Five years after Mark Twain's book appeared, a young Englishman came to Giza and began the work which would transform Egyptology for ever.

CHAPTER EIGHT

EGYPTOLOGY COMES OF AGE

FROM TREASURE HUNT TO SCIENCE

SIR WILLIAM MATTHEW FLINDERS PETRIE (1853–1942) is often referred to as the father of modern Egyptology. One of his disciples once wrote that 'When Petrie began his career, Herodotus was our only guide to the history of Egypt; when he ended that career, the whole of Egyptian prehistory and history had been mapped out and settled.' This may be hyperbole, but it is understandable hyperbole. Thanks to the care and rigour of his methods, the ingenuity of his approach to problems both small and large, and perhaps above all to his sheer energy, Flinders Petrie brought order out of chaos and – even though some of his methods were later superseded – changed for good the way archaeology was conducted.

He wrote over a hundred books and more than a thousand articles; he dug or surveyed at more than fifty sites, not only in Egypt, Sinai and Palestine but also at home in Britain. He stressed, for the first time, the need to make meticulous records of everything found at a dig, no matter how insignificant it might appear at the time. He showed the importance of collecting, classifying and noting pottery and other apparently trifling objects. He was a shrewd recruiter of young talent, and trained all his followers in his methods; years later, they all hailed him as a great teacher. To cite another verdict on his career: 'He found archaeology in Egypt a treasure hunt; he left it a science.'

THE INFLUENCE OF PIAZZI SMYTH

It is a curious quirk of history that the book which first inspired the scientifically minded young Petrie in his chosen vocation was one of the texts most derided by archaeologists and admired by mystics: the Scottish astronomer Charles Piazzi Smyth's *Our Inheritance in the Great Pyramid* (see page 168). Petrie read it when he was just thirteen, was fascinated by its suggestion that the nature of ancient measurement systems might be deduced from the accurate study of surviving monuments, and resolved to travel to the Pyramid to survey the whole thing for himself. Young Petrie had acquired the book from his father, William Petrie senior, a friend and later a 'disciple' of Piazzi Smyth, and also a fervent Christian fundamentalist.

In Piazzi Smyth's writings, Petrie's father thought he saw what many anxious Christians were seeking in this generation: a means of reconciling scripture with the increasingly damaging accounts of the world produced by Darwin and the geologists. Petrie's father was so inspired by the *Pyramid* book that he set about perfecting a series of theodolites, sextants and verniers for the great task of journeying to Egypt and confirming Piazzi Smyth's convictions, but for some reason – although he had even advanced so far in his travel arrangements as to design a portable case for his false teeth – had never quite got around to leaving England. Driven partly by impatience, partly by his own passion, the younger Petrie would carry out the mission his father looked likely to postpone for ever.

Flinders Petrie had an unconventional childhood, and, with the exception of a brief evening course in algebra and trigonometry which he took at the age of twenty-four, received no formal education whatsoever. His father raised him to follow his own severe faith, and explained to him the literal truth of the scriptures. A sickly child, Petrie was forbidden all outdoor games and spent most of his time in the house, in the company of adults. But he had an active, inquiring mind, and although his flair was for science rather than languages – he taught himself geometry from Euclid, just for the fun of it – he was delighted at finding a copy of Spineto's *Lectures on Hieroglyphics* and spent many happy hours copying its figures. He was six.

Soon, the boy had added geology, magnetism (on which he wrote a small treatise), astronomy, coin collecting, chemistry and surveying to his list of enthusiasms. Father and son worked happily together at mapping ancient earthworks and stone circles, including, in 1874, the greatest of all British ruins: Stonehenge. Between that date and 1880 Petrie made some ten similar expeditions on his own, mapping many different sites in southern England and completing the unfinished Stonehenge investigation. By 1877 his activities had drawn the respectful interest of the Royal Archaeological Institute, and he was allowed to spend many absorbed hours in the British Museum's various collections. The result of this work was a precociously learned book, *Inductive Metrology, or the Recovery of Ancient Measurements from the Monuments* (1887) – a work of great originality which soon became a standard text.

In the midst of all this strenuous activity Petrie became an ever more fervent and vocal supporter of the Piazzi Smyth view, aligning himself with biblical fundamentalists and calling the Great Pyramid 'the grandest writing on earth'. His first proper book, published in 1874, was entitled *Researches on the Great Pyramid*. It was a ringing defence of Piazzi Smyth against the scoffers, although he did differ sufficiently from the astronomer on enough key points to be regarded as something of a heretic. Petrie was not, for example, persuaded, as Piazzi Smyth certainly was, that the British were descended from the Lost Tribes of Israel. Relations with Piazzi Smyth grew noticeably cooler from this point on.

PETRIE STARTS WORK AT GIZA

The Petries decided it was time for independent action and threw themselves into preparations for the journey to Egypt. Petrie junior took time off only to do some voluntary research for what would eventually become the *Oxford English Dictionary* before sailing from Liverpool on the SS *Nephthys* in November 1880. His father promised to follow a week or so later. He did not.

At first, young Petrie suffered dreadfully from sea-sickness and was obliged to sleep on deck. But he recovered quickly and soon made the overland journey first from Alexandria to Cairo

Flinders Petrie, the father of modern Egyptology.

and then from Cairo to Giza, where he set up home in an abandoned tomb. His plan was to work uninterruptedly throughout the winter months and to be done by spring, when the first hordes of tourists would begin their annual invasion. Always spartan in his habits, Petrie soon came to like his primitive quarters, despite the presence of many small, uninvited guests: 'Did not get any sleep till 11 or 12, and then broken by (1st) trap down, big rat, killed and reset. (2nd) mouse about trap for long, though bait must be eaten, got up to see; (3rd) fleas. (4th) mouse let trap down without going in; got up; reset it; (5th) mouse got in, got up, killed him, reset trap; (6th) Fleas; (7th) Dog set up protracted conversational barking ....'

But inconveniences of this kind did nothing to dampen his enthusiasm. He thrived on the lack of convention out there on the plateau, dressing scruffily, letting his beard and hair grow unkempt, sleeping when he felt like it, and enjoying his very basic diet of rice, tomatoes, eggs and the occasional tinned pilchard, with fresh oranges from Cairo to fend off scurvy. He suffered badly from sore throats and other ailments, but in other respects was healthier than he had ever been – no longer a sickly boy, but a sturdy and indefatigable young explorer.

His first priority was to carry out the most accurate possible triangulation of the whole Giza site, using a first-rate 10-inch (25 cm) theodolite and a ×35 telescope. He worked with extreme care, checking and rechecking each angle as many as fourteen times from some fifty basic stations, while his assistant Ali Gabri held a parasol over the theodolite to keep it from expanding in the heat. At the close of day Petrie would retreat to his tomb, write up his measurements and listen to the eerie tunes played on the flute by Mohammed, an employee of Ali Gabri, who had been hired as a nocturnal bodyguard and lived in the next tomb.

Petrie was thrilled by his findings. Estimating that his own degree of error in measurement was never greater than a quarter of an inch (6 mm), and often not greater than a tenth of an inch (2.5 mm), he was awed by the accuracy of the Pyramid's construction, calling it 'a triumph of skill. Its errors, both in lengths and in angles, could be covered by placing one's thumb on them.'

Realizing that his work would not be done by the time the tourists started to arrive, he changed his tactics and extended the scope of his dig, leaving for a summer in England in June 1881, returning in October and continuing work until the early summer of 1882. Turning his attention now from the exterior to the interior, he got his workmen to clear all the muck and rubble from the base of the descending passage: they did so by forming a human chain, passing full baskets up and empty baskets down. Meanwhile, Petrie did his best to scare off as many tourists as he could by wandering around dressed in nothing but his bright pink underwear – a tactic which usually worked with the ladies, at any rate.

At sundown, when the noisy nuisances had left, Petrie would re-enter the Pyramid, still hot from the fierce daytime sun and choked with churned-up dust which gave him terrible headaches. Here he would work at his measurements until deep into the night, sometimes until dawn. When it was unbearably hot, he worked naked. Using his special chains and other instruments, some of which permitted him accuracy to within $1/100$ and even $1/1000$ inch, Petrie drew up the truest estimate to date of the Pyramid's inner workings. Among other findings, he established that the average error in the masonry was a trifling $1/50$ inch over 150 feet (45 metres); he confirmed that the King's Chamber was a triumph of geometry, the ratio of its length to the circuit of its side wall being the same as the ratio of 1 to *pi* (approximately $22/7$, or 3.14285...); and that the exterior of the Pyramid had also been built according to the same *pi* proportion. On the other hand, he also discovered some surprisingly clumsy work in parts, noting that the granite in the King's Antechamber was not merely unfinished but even partially defective.

Understandably elated by these discoveries, Petrie once again turned his attention to the exterior, trying to locate more casing stones of the kind that had been unearthed by the explosives of Colonel Vyse. The task was arduous and hazardous – more often than not, rubble would immediately slide back down into the pits dug by his workers, and at one point he was almost killed. Courage and endurance brought their rewards: before too long, he had unearthed not only more of the 15-ton limestone casing blocks, but enough of the Pyramid's actual base to make measurement possible. Once again, he was profoundly impressed by the accuracy of the Egyptian masons. The stones had been cut so precisely and fitted so exactly that the thin layer of mortar between them was, on average, about the thickness of a fingernail – about $\frac{1}{50}$ inch. He also found that the mean variation of the casings from a perfectly straight line was about $\frac{1}{100}$ inch over a distance of 75 inches (1.9 metres). 'Merely to place such stones in exact contact would be careful work,' he wrote, 'but to do so with cement in the joint seems almost impossible: it is to be compared with the finest opticians' work on a scale of acres.'

Possibly the most important of all Petrie's discoveries on this unprecedentedly rigorous excavation was an observation which may seem a little on the technical side, but which had enormous consequences for Piazzi Smyth's case. Trusting the evidence of his eyes and instruments over the authority of Piazzi Smyth, Petrie was forced to conclude – and he bolstered his conclusion with overwhelmingly powerful evidence – that the true base length of the Pyramid had to be judged not from the sockets which marked its four cornerstones but from the edge of the pavement, some 20 inches (50 cm) higher. Instead of measuring 9140 British inches (232.15 metres) as Smyth had contended, the true base line was rather shorter – 9069 inches (230.35 metres).

This discrepancy demolished all of Smyth's calculations – for example, his estimate that the Pyramid encoded the 365 days of the year. With Petrie's revised figures, that sum now read 362.76 – not nearly so impressive a fit. Petrie also demonstrated that the unit of measurement on which the Pyramid was built must have been the 'royal cubit' of 20.63 inches (52.4 cm), which results in a base line of 440 cubits and a height of 280 cubits.

The Royal Society granted Petrie £100 to publish his results as *The Pyramids and Temples of Gizeh* in 1883. It was a triumph, although one which he regarded in a slightly rueful spirit, noting that when he had read Smyth's inspiring book as a boy, he had had no premonition that it would be he who 'would reach the ugly little fact which killed the beautiful theory'. The sequel, *The Great Pyramid*, appeared a decade later.

Petrie's investigation of the Great Pyramid was more than enough accomplishment for one lifetime, yet it was only the beginning of a career which lasted an astonishing six decades longer. In 1892 he became the holder of Britain's first Egyptological chair, at University College, London, and retained that post until 1933; the Petrie Museum, one of the finest of its kind in the world, is still housed within the University's precincts in Bloomsbury.

His influence on subsequent generations was incalculable – one of his disciples, incidentally, being a young classicist called T. E. Lawrence, who was later to be known as Lawrence of Arabia. Lawrence wrote a lively, humorous account of his time with Petrie in letters home ('... tinned kidneys mingle with mummy-corpses and amulets in the soup: my bed is all gritty with prehistoric alabaster jars of unique types – and my feet at night keep the bread-box from rats ...'); he stressed his mentor's energy, his feverish rate of speech, and his dogmatism tempered with great good humour.

T. E. Lawrence – 'Lawrence of Arabia' – was one of Flinders Petrie's disciples.

With Petrie's career, the story of travellers to the Great Pyramid is in essence if not in detail almost complete. After Petrie, and notwithstanding the best efforts of the 'pyramidiots', the golden age of colourful rogues, freebooters, soldiers, monomaniacs and poets gives way to a more prosaic age, dominated by the scientists on one wing and the tourists (better behaved now than their rowdy Victorian forebears) on the other. Thanks to the scientists, we now know more about the Pyramid than Petrie ever did. And yet it would be fair to say that all the subsequent researchers of the twentieth and twenty-first centuries are in his debt, and aspire – with the help of new technologies – to the great Petrie ideal of accuracy and fidelity above all things. When he published his memoirs, Petrie had the cover embossed with five hieroglyphic characters – a motto derived from Akhnaten and meaning: 'Living in Truth'.

AFTER PETRIE

The major advances since Petrie's time can be divided into two main waves, the first lasting from about 1902 when Gaston Maspero, the successor to Auguste Mariette, divided up the rights to excavate the Giza plateau along national lines, until the 1930s, after which expeditions began gradually to tail off in response to the European political situation. World War II then put paid to all such activities for several years.

One of the earliest followers in Petrie's path was also one of the most important: the American Egyptologist George Andrew Reisner (1867–1942). A slow and meticulous worker, who left much of his research unpublished, Reisner made many significant discoveries in the field of pyramids, notably in Lower Nubia where he uncovered the pyramids of sixty-eight Ethiopian kings. This most remarkable find was made in the course of his excavations at Giza. He was working on the valley temple of Menkaure when, on 2 February 1925, he discovered – more or less by happy chance – the tomb of Queen Hetepheres, Khufu's mother (see Chapter 4). It was also in 1925 that an engineer, J. H. Cole, carried out a survey of the Great Pyramid that exceeded even Petrie's brilliant work in its accuracy.

After World War II there was a fresh wave of exploration which has continued to the present day. Between 1963 and 1975 two Italian archaeologists carried out the first complete survey of all surviving pyramids of the Old and Middle Kingdoms, publishing their results in eight large volumes. The technique of radio-carbon dating started to be applied to the sites, and in some cases led to chronologies being altered by as much as four hundred years or more. In 1986 the Great Pyramid was subjected to a microgravimetric test, designed to determine its exact density at different levels – a test which led to some excited talk about a possible 'hidden chamber' near the Queen's Chamber. Romantics will be sad to hear that it appears more likely that the anomaly is due to layers of less dense rocks surrounding the core masonry.

Of all the other expeditions, including one to measure air pollution, the most famous is undoubtedly that organized by a German team in 1992, in the course of which the robotics engineer Rudolf Gantenbrink sent small, remote-controlled cameras up into the shafts from the King's and Queen's Chambers. The discovery in the latter of a limestone plug, often grandly referred to in fringe literature as a 'door', with copper pins projecting from it has been a godsend to new generations of pyramidologists and 'pyramidiots' – the subject of Chapter 9.

THE 'BLACK EGYPT' ARGUMENT

So far we have mainly been concerned with the Western discovery – in fact, of course, a rediscovery – of the pyramids and the civilization which produced them. In recent decades, however, some writers have wished to wrest these matters from white Europeans and Americans and reclaim the legacy of Egypt for modern people of African descent – particularly for African-Americans, since it is in the United States that this movement has found its home. Some of the claims associated with this movement have been extravagant, and it is easy for orthodox scholars to dismiss such works as simply a new mode of crankery, inspired this time by racial politics rather than religious mania.

This is a delicate area, and one in which it is important not to rush to judgement. No doubt much of the literature in this field is recklessly composed and lacks the protocols of mainstream academic argument, since much of it takes the form of self-published pamphlets and manifestos passed from hand to hand. But is it always, therefore, without serious content? The most prominent (and more or less mainstream) study to regard this line of argument with uncondescending sympathy, if not absolute agreement, is Martin Bernal's much-discussed *Black Athena* (Vol. I, 1987). This is a stimulating and passionate work which, even if

An American transport plane flying over the Giza pyramids in 1943 with supplies for the Allied troops in North Africa. All excavations on the plateau were stopped for the duration of World War II.

A Spanish engraving from 1862 depicting black Africans building the pyramids.

derided by many specialists, has had the salutary effect of making many readers re-examine their assumptions and sometimes discover unwarranted beliefs of which they had previously been quite unaware.

Bernal is a shrewd observer of all those forces, from scholarly rigour to mere snobbery or worse, which determine whether or not a theory is beyond the intellectual pale. He records the difficulty he had in persuading his university's library even to stock a copy of one of the most venerable contributions in this field, G. G. M. James's *Stolen Legacy* (its full title continues: *The Greeks were not the authors of Greek Philosophy, but the people of North Africa, commonly called the Egyptians*), so set were the librarians against the notion that it counted as a proper book.

A highly respected academic and at the same time an unwelcome trespasser into other people's areas of expertise, Bernal has not merely immersed himself in the 'Black Egypt' arguments but has thought deeply about the sociology of knowledge – about, that is, 'what differentiates fruitful radical innovation from sterile crankiness'. It is his contention that, however unconventional its presentation, much of the African-American revisionist work cannot fairly be dismissed out of hand as cranky, since it does not fall into the defining vice of cranks, who tend 'to add new unknown and unknowable factors into their theories: lost continents, men from outer space, planetary collisions, etc.' Which is, of course, precisely the area in which many recent best-selling writers on Egypt have specialized. We are about to enter the world of the Egyptological mystic and the Egyptological crank – the realm, that is, of the pyramidologists and 'pyramidiots'.

CHAPTER NINE

PYRAMIDOLOGY, HERETICS, MYSTICS AND CRANKS

IT IS A TRUTH UNIVERSALLY ACKNOWLEDGED THAT, while the subject of ancient Egypt has undoubtedly attracted some of the finest, most disinterested and most rigorous intellects of the past few centuries, it has also been a magnet for all manner of obsessives, charlatans, occultists and cranks. Professional Egyptologists have an unkind name for such types: 'pyramidiots'. One can well understand their irritation at seeing how all the countless painstaking hours that have built their discipline up into a genuine fund of accurate knowledge and scrupulous procedures may simply be cast to the wind by some raving visionary who claims that he was told in a dream that the pyramids were built by Venusians.

And yet, looking back at the long, motley history of the Egyptian rediscovery, the boundaries of sense and folly are a little more disputed than this clear division might suggest. At least a few of the greatest of the scholars involved in creating Egyptology (including its acknowledged modern paterfamilias, Petrie, in his pious adolescence) had some brush with occult theories, and in the period up to the seventeenth century, or even later, it is not easy to draw a line between orthodox and unorthodox belief, between science and magic. Witness the case of Sir Isaac Newton: probably the greatest of all scientists, but by the standards of the twenty-first century none the less a clear victim of 'pyramidiocy'.

For many centuries, one central Egyptological belief could be shared both by scholars of the highest intelligence and by those barely one step away from the lunatic asylum – the faith in a Lost Knowledge: the idea, in other words, that the Egyptians were in possession of all manner of wonderful secret insights and techniques, which were transmitted to posterity only in mutilated fragments – or not at all – by their conquerors and successors on the world stage, the Greeks and Romans. The Great Quest was, therefore, to rediscover the said Lost Knowledge; and few of those engaged in the quest, then as now, could resist the temptation posed by that vast brooding object on the Giza plateau and its two younger siblings.

This chapter, then, will rapidly survey some of the wilder shores of pyramidological studies over the nineteenth and twentieth centuries. Not everyone mentioned deserves to be dismissed as a fool or a charlatan (although quite a number can), but the reader should be wary throughout of taking any of their contentions too seriously without a full knowledge of the orthodox opinion on such matters – opinion which is, however the occultists may jeer, either the truth, or at any rate the best approximation to it that human ingenuity can afford. Thus braced, let us board the merry-go-round with a colourful but wholly sincere and useful character.

G. B. CAVIGLIA

Giovanni Battista Caviglia (1770–1845) has a foot in both worlds of scholarship, orthodox and unorthodox. Unlike most pyramidologists of later generations, he actually made some genuine contributions towards the understanding of Khufu's structure. On the other hand, like many others, he was fond of claiming that his researches had put him in touch with great, dark mysteries. An English gentleman who met Caviglia in Cairo, Alexander William Crawford (1812–80; later ennobled as Lord Lindsay), was impressed by the Italian's authentic Christian piety, but perturbed by his hints about the superhuman experiences that had come his way. As Crawford wrote home to England, 'Caviglia told me that he had pushed his studies in magic, animal magnetism, etc, to an extent which had nearly killed him ... to the very verge, he said, of what it is forbidden man to know, and it was only the purity of his intentions which saved him.' Possibly so; though it cannot be said that 'purity' was the hallmark of Caviglia in his other dealings.

A Genoese merchant seaman who gave up the sea to pursue what he saw as the 'mystery' of the Great Pyramid, Caviglia had originally arrived in Egypt as the master of a Maltese vessel, flying under a British flag. He then moved not just to his ancient goal but right into it, setting up home in Davison's Chamber, once he had cleared it of its thick and slimy coating of bat droppings. One account of his new home described it as being transformed into a 'residential apartment', although few dwellings worthy of that description have a ceiling that is only 3 feet (1 metre) high. Caviglia then set about investigating his new home, financing himself by helping other Europeans to loot everything they fancied from the rest of the Giza necropolis.

Caviglia was convinced that there must be more secret chambers to discover, and did a great deal of damage to the area surrounding Davison's Chamber before he gave up. He then made the perilous descent into the 'well' from the Grand Gallery, and found, like Davison before him, that its base was plugged with sand and rocks. Managing to persuade his reluctant workers to make the same descent, he started to excavate this rubbish and to haul up buckets of debris, but after a while – lungs clogged with dust and the powder of dried bat dung – they rebelled at the sheer unpleasantness of the task, and work was stopped.

He then tried a new tack, and began to clear the lower reaches of the descending passage. Brave to the point of foolhardiness, Caviglia crawled down

the cleared space for about 150 feet (46 metres), at which point the air became so thick with dust and muck and the heat so bad that he began to spit up blood. He persisted, however, and went another 50 feet (15 metres) deeper, at which point he noticed what looked like a doorway leading into a hole. Cajoling his men back to work, he hacked away at this wall until a shower of dust and small rocks fell around them and they felt a sudden blast of cooler air. As the dust cleared, they also discovered ropes and baskets – their own ropes and baskets. They had uncovered the blocked-off connection between the descending passage and the 'well'.

At this point, Caviglia was unexpectedly joined by a much wealthier explorer – Colonel Howard Vyse. The colonel was so impressed by what this curious Italian told him about the occult purposes for which the Pyramid had been built that he threw his considerable fortune into advancing these researches, and employed Caviglia as his superintendent of works. All went swimmingly until Vyse found out that Caviglia was mainly using the new, expanded workforce to further his other concerns, raiding the nearby burial pits for everything from scarab rings to mummies – the powdered flesh of mummies still being popular in some European medical circles as a supposedly sure-fire cure for fractures and other ailments.

The pair parted on bad terms, and Caviglia, sulking, went off to Paris where he managed from time to time to win the patronage of another famous British antiquity-hunter, Lord Elgin. Whatever hermetic 'secrets' Caviglia had gleaned in addition to his genuine archaeological finds, they were manifestly not of the order to bring worldly riches in their train. Yet he was probably as sincere as he was courageous and determined; and the men who soon followed him in search of ancient wisdom were, beyond question, all sincere to a fault.

JOHN TAYLOR

If there is one prevailing theme which unites almost every 'alternative' (or 'crank') theory about the Great Pyramid, no matter what its other details are, it is that the dimensions of the building, both exterior and interior, enshrine some form of Egyptian higher wisdom – geometrical, astronomical, geographical and what have you. Rumours and legends to this effect are of considerable antiquity, but the modern craze for such speculative computations began with a modest English man of letters who never actually travelled to Giza himself.

Opposite

Satellite view of the Giza plateau. Khufu's Pyramid is at the bottom left of the picture.

John Taylor (1781–1864), a poet, essayist and sometime editor of the *London Observer*, was in his fifties when he first caught the Pyramid bug, and devoted much of the remaining three decades of his life to collecting and collating information about the building's nature. Taylor summed up his arguments in *The Great Pyramid: Why Was It Built & Who Built It?*, published in 1859.

John Taylor with a model of the Great Pyramid.

He was clear-eyed enough to note the considerable discrepancies in figures that had been coming back to Europe since the time of Greaves, and imaginative enough to grasp that the increasing length of the base in these reports must be due to the progressive clearing away of rubble and the exposure of still deeper layers of masonry. Taking Howard Vyse's figures as the most accurate available, he set about trying to interpret them.

Following a hint from Herodotus, Taylor applied himself to the question of why the builders had chosen the angle of roughly 51 degrees for the Pyramid's faces, instead of the more standard 60 degrees as in an equilateral triangle. A leap of imagination prompted him to divide the perimeter of the Pyramid's base line by a figure equal to twice its height. The result: 3.144 – tantalizingly close to, though not precisely the same as, *pi*: 3.14159... and so on. Concluding that this was unlikely to be coincidence, and hunting around for other implications, Taylor eventually hit on the notion that the base perimeter was meant to represent the circumference of the earth at the equator, while the height represented the distance from the earth's centre to the pole. If so, this would corroborate Jomard's contention that the Egyptians had been able accurately to calculate a geographical degree; and to multiply it by 360 to arrive at the circumference of the earth; and to use *pi* to calculate its radius. In Taylor's words, the Egyptians 'knew the earth was a sphere; and by observing the motion of the heavenly bodies over the earth's surface, had ascertained its circumference, and were desirous of leaving behind them a record of the circumference as correct and imperishable as it was possible for them to construct'.

Taylor's next self-appointed task was to improve on Greaves and Isaac Newton by determining the unit of measurement employed by the Egyptians, working on the assumption that one part of the *pi* ratio would almost certainly have been expressed as a whole number rather than as an inelegant fraction. Trial and error led him to the proportion of 366 to 116.5. This rang a bell: 366 is a decent approximation to the number of days in the solar year. He played around with this figure, and found that if he used simple British inches as his unit, then the perimeter was – again not perfectly, but as a satisfactory approximation – 366 × 100.

It so happened that the great English astronomer Herschel had recently proposed a unit only fractionally larger than the British inch as the one best suited to reflect the actual dimensions of the earth – he rejected the French metre on the grounds that it ignored the fact that the earth is not a perfect sphere, and was miscalculated anyway. The British Ordnance Survey had fixed the axis of the earth from pole to pole as 7898.78 miles, or almost 500,500,000 inches. Simply boost the length of the inch by a hairsbreadth to make an exact 500 million inches. Fifty of these units would give a terrestrial yard; half that number a cubit.

Taylor was delighted by the coincidence of Herschel's calculations with his own pyramidical conclusions. He was equally pleased with another set of data which hinted that Newton's postulation of a 'sacred' cubit of about 25 inches (63.5 cm) was correct and – Taylor thought – showed that the good old British inch was even older than people assumed: the relic, no less, of an ancient unit of measure based on the true dimensions of the earth, and thus known to the Egyptians, too. He threw himself into a tireless study of all known measurement systems from around the world, and went back to his models of the Pyramid with renewed fervour.

At around this point, however, Taylor's faith in geometry and history collided headlong with his religious faith. Convinced, like many pious men of his day, of the literal truth of the Old Testament, he was certain that the universe had been created about four thousand years earlier and that the world had been drowned in a great Flood around 2400 BC. At this point in the mid-nineteenth century, Khufu's Pyramid was assumed to date from about 2100 BC. So how, Taylor agonized, could mankind have redeveloped so rapidly in a mere three hundred years? Not having had the benefit of reading the best-sellers of Erich Von Däniken about meddlesome space beings (see page 176), he grasped at the only compromise available to him: the Pyramid had been divinely inspired.

It was probable, he asserted, that to some human beings in the earliest ages of society, a degree of intellectual power was given by the Creator, which raised them far above the level of those succeeding inhabitants of the earth. He went further. Since the venerable British inch was so close to the 'Pyramid inch' as to suggest that it was one and the same unit, slightly worn down by generations of transmission, was it not apparent that the British must be related to the Lost Tribes of Israel? Alas, to his bitter disappointment Taylor realized that his marvellous discoveries were being treated at best with caution, at worst with sheer indifference, by most of his contemporaries; the Royal Society, whose members were Britain's most eminent men of science, politely declined his offer to address them on the subject of the Pyramid. He was in danger of dying a sad man, until his cause was suddenly taken up at the eleventh hour by a man too eminent to be ignored.

CHARLES PIAZZI SMYTH

Charles Piazzi Smyth was Astronomer Royal for Scotland and believed in the 'sacred cubit'.

The last weeks of Taylor's life were sweetened by an intense correspondence with the Scottish scientist, then in his early forties, whom we encountered briefly in Chapter 8 as an early influence on Flinders Petrie. Charles Piazzi Smyth (1819–1900) had studied Taylor's calculations, and thought that there was something in them. Remembered by orthodox science for his work in spectroscopy, and as Astronomer Royal of Scotland, Piazzi Smyth was also convinced that the British had inherited the 'Pyramid inch' or 'sacred inch', calculated as being $\frac{1}{25}$ of a 'sacred cubit' – the primary unit used by Noah for his Ark, Moses for his Tabernacle and the Egyptians for the Pyramid.

On Taylor's death, Piazzi Smyth resolved to go to Egypt and confirm or explode the older man's conjectures for good. He set out with his wife in December 1864, and despite meeting with all manner of setbacks, from shortage of funds at home to chaos and galloping inflation in Egypt, eventually made it to Cairo. (They hated it: the smells, the flies, the noise, the squalor.) Still, the couple were generously received by the viceroy, Ismail Pasha, although not so generously that he would consent to the Englishman's request for full backing for an excavation: hardly surprising, since Piazzi Smyth wanted to clear the entire base area, to bore assorted holes and so on.

Instead, the viceroy granted him twenty workers for the site and the means of transport to it. By late January 1865, Piazzi Smyth's team had cleaned up the interior rooms and passages of Khufu's Pyramid – often fouled by tourists, or (in the case of the passage uncovered by Caviglia) craftily reblocked by lazy tour guides who did not like the effort involved in making the descent – enough for an extended visit inside to be bearable. He set to work with a measuring bar, 105 inches (2.67 metres) long and furnished with thermometers at each end to register any change of heat large enough to expand it, and with other measuring instruments of equal delicacy. He also brought along a camera, and exposed some eighty plates using a magnesium flare system of his own devising.

Outside, he used cords, sextants, theodolites and telescopes, all of the best quality and latest design. To measure the latitude, he went to the very top of the Pyramid with his plumb-line and stayed there with his wife for several successive nights, heedless of vertigo. He used his telescope to make accurate observations of the stars. He called on the services of two fellow Scots, honest engineers who happened to be passing, to help him uncover once again the sockets at the corners of the Pyramid's base, previously cleared by the French expedition but now once again covered with sand, rocks and rubbish. To his chagrin he had to leave the two men to complete the task on their own, since four months had now elapsed and the Piazzi Smyths' return journey had been booked long in advance.

Back home in Scotland, he worked at collating all his measurements, augmenting them with the figures sent to him by his new friends – who estimated the base length at 9110 inches (231.4 metres), a figure much shorter than the one Taylor had used. His conclusions were complex, but a few of them stand out. He claimed, for example, that the ceremonial completion of the Pyramid must have occurred at midnight on the autumnal equinox of 2170 BC, when the star *Alpha Draconis* was exactly visible along the line of the descending passage and the chief star of the Pleiades, *n-Tauri*, was crossing the vertical meridian of the Pyramid, directly above the upper limit of the Grand Gallery.

More impressively, Piazzi Smyth confirmed that the mean angle of the Pyramid's faces was just over 51 degree 51 minutes, and put this together with a mean base line (using the measurements of both Colonel Vyse and the French) of 763.81. Repeating Taylor's earlier calculation, he came up with 3.141259... an astonishingly precise approximation to *pi*, much more impressive than the figure of 3.144 which had so inspired Taylor in the first place. And so on. Piazzi Smyth felt that he had been vindicated: the Pyramid *did* incorporate a scale model of the earth, its base perimeter *did* correspond with the number of days in the solar year, and it *was* built with an advanced knowledge of geometry.

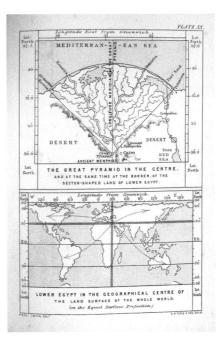

Two plates from Piazzi Smyth's *Our Inheritance in the Great Pyramid* showing (*above left*) sections of the Grand Gallery and (*above right*) the Great Pyramid in the 'geographical centre of the land surface of the whole world'.

Naturally, Piazzi Smyth was more than pleased by his results, and so, at first, were his peers: he was awarded a gold medal for his work by the Edinburgh Royal Society. But doubts soon began to be raised, grumbles were voiced, and when he finally wrote up all his conclusions in the huge, three-volume *Life and Work at the Great Pyramid of Jeezah during the Months of January, February, March and April, A.D. 1865*, the reception was not nearly so kind. In fact, it was often openly scornful.

For most of Piazzi Smyth's readers, the problem was neither the accuracy of his measurements nor the correctness of his mathematics, but the purpose to which they were put. The controversy surrounding Charles Darwin's *The Origin of Species*, which had been published in 1859 and contended that mankind had not descended from a Biblical Adam but had evolved through a process of natural selection, was still raging. Like Darwin's opponents, Piazzi Smyth and Taylor were Christians of the most literal-minded, fundamentalist kind. Faced with the same intellectual quandaries as Taylor about Creation and the Flood, Piazzi Smyth had found the same explanation – the Pyramid was divinely inspired. The sceptics and the wits had a field day. To make matters worse, the waters of argument become muddied when a notional supporter of Piazzi Smyth's called Robert Menzies – the kind of intellectual 'friend' to make anyone yearn for a good, straightforward enemy – jumped into the fray with his contention that the Pyramid was not only divinely inspired but contained a literal prophecy in stone, with each 'Pyramid inch' of its internal passage system corresponding to a year in the history of the world, from Creation to Apocalypse.

Seemingly immune to the worst sneers of informed and ignorant critics alike, Piazzi Smyth proceeded to carry his calculations and speculations to still more extraordinary degrees. He worked out, for example, that the Pyramid rises from its base in the proportion of 10 units of height to 9 units of width. Now, taking the height of the Pyramid and multiplying it by 10 to the power of 9, he came up with the (adjusted) figure of 91,840,000 miles – an approximation to the average distance of the earth from the sun. This calculation is still a key part of the annals of pyramidology.

Wonderful stuff; but the problem was that even Piazzi Smyth's careful figures were no better than a fair estimate of the exterior dimensions of the Pyramid, and as long as so much as a few inches of uncertainty remained in those figures – which would be the case until someone cleared away the entire base area – the Taylor/Piazzi Smyth case would remain nothing more than a charming set of hypotheses. As we saw in Chapter 8, one of the quieter ironies of this history is that it was a good Christian and sincere admirer of Piazzi Smyth, Flinders Petrie, who eventually carried out the work which, designed to prove the 'Pyramid inch' and all its related stories, actually blew it to smithereens. But the next of our pyramidologists took a journey of faith in quite the other direction.

DAVID DAVIDSON

A structural engineer from Leeds read Menzies's 'prophetic' case, found it vastly irritating and, like the sound rational agnostic he was, began to gather together the data which would scupper it. Unfortunately, the more deeply David Davidson read in Pyramid literature, the more persuaded he became that it was he, not Menzies, who had been on the wrong track. With all the fervour of the fresh convert, he declared to the world – or that part of it which would listen – that the Pyramid was all that Taylor, Piazzi Smyth and Menzies had claimed it to be, and more. It was, he said, a proof in stone that the Bible was indeed the work of God.

Much of Davidson's work recapitulates earlier claims that the Pyramid's measurements were founded on knowledge of, and tacitly represent, the dimensions of the earth and its orbit around the sun. The new aspect of his writings responded to a phenomenon which Petrie had noticed but not used as the basis for any theory – the fact that each of the Pyramid's sides is very slightly concave, an effect invisible to the naked eye from most angles, and later shown up quite clearly by aerial photography. Davidson used this detail as the basis for an ingenious set of calculations by which he hoped to prove that the Pyramid represented the three different methods of measuring the earth's annual rotation around the sun (the solar, the sidereal and the anomalistic) that had been found useful by modern astronomers.

Madame Helena Blavatsky, a founder of the Theosophy movement, photographed in London in 1889.

It might not seem a very radical point – nor, indeed, a particularly persuasive one – but Davidson built on this and related arguments to bolster his case that, since the Egyptians 'obviously' knew both the exact length of the sidereal year and the distance of the earth from the sun, they also potentially had access to knowledge of everything from the specific gravity of the earth to the speed of light. They had access to knowledge, in other words, not merely as complex as that of nineteenth-century science – roughly the Taylor/Piazzi Smyth position – but vastly in excess of it. 'It has taken man,' Davidson concluded, 'thousands of years to discover by experiment what he knew originally by a surer and simpler method.' Moreover, 'It means that the whole empirical basis of modern civilization is a makeshift collection of hypotheses compared with the Natural Law basis of that civilization of the past.' For Davidson, the old, old question of why the pyramids were built had a simple answer. They were built to preserve a highly advanced form of natural science through a coming Dark Age, until such a time as human beings were once again advanced enough to decode its teachings and come again into the full knowledge that they had once enjoyed.

Whether or not the Pyramid encoded prophetic truths, it did not take any great gifts of prophecy to predict what would come next. However much the mathematicians, astronomers, archaeologists and Egyptologists might try to resist his wild surmises, Davidson had unleashed a vast, murky and unstoppable flood of 'pyramidiocy' and related nonsense, which has not ebbed away even today.

To provide details of all the madcap, mathematically based theories which have grown from Davidson (and Menzies, Piazzi Smyth and Taylor) would be a long and tiresome task. But it is worth mentioning one or two of Davidson's more flavoursome successors, such as Morton Edgar (who 'read' in the Pyramid the prediction that, by the year 2914, the end of the thousand-year 'Day of Judgement', humankind will have experienced the full benefit of the sacrificial work of Christ, and will regain that perfect human nature which Father Adam lost in the beginning of his disobedience 7040 years previously); or Colonel J. Garnier (who discovered a prophecy that in 1920 the rivers of the world would all turn into blood). The school of pyramidal mathematics, too, is a very long way from being dead. A prime recent example is Peter Lemesurier's *The Great Pyramid Decoded* (1977 and 1997), which is so laden with page after page of exhaustive calculations as to deter all but the sternest of seekers after truth.

It is time to examine some of the other fringes. An exhaustive survey of all the quaint and curious (non-mathematical, non-predictive) things that have been asserted or believed about the Great Pyramid would not merely be dull but would risk inducing odd states of mind into the most robust browser. For the sake of both brevity and sanity, three principal tendencies may be identified: the Occultists, the Atlanteans, and the Extra-Terrestrials.

THE OCCULTISTS

From the early eighteenth century all manner of secret societies and cults, from the Rosicrucians to the Freemasons, seized eagerly on the trappings (often poorly understood) of ancient Egyptian culture and religion, either by way of conferring a kind of instant antiquity on their invented practices, or in more extreme cases claiming direct succession from Egyptian priesthoods. For these groups, the Great Pyramid often figured as the mythical Place of Initiation – the site where the acolyte was admitted into the full light of those Ancient Secrets that had been carefully guarded and passed down over the centuries.

The cults that followed in the late nineteenth and early twentieth centuries often did just the same, the most obvious instance being that of the synthetic belief system which called itself Theosophy. One of the founders of the movement, Helena Petrovna Blavatsky, usually referred to as Madame Blavatsky (1831–91), went through a major Egyptian craze – although she later shifted her

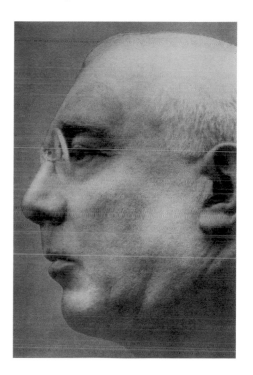

P. D. Ouspensky photographed in 1935, a year after publishing an account of his experiences at the Great Pyramid on the eve of World War I.

enthusiasm to Tibet – and in her works *The Secret Doctrine* (1888) and *Isis Unveiled* (1877) instructed her disciples that the Pyramid was 'the everlasting record and the indestructible symbol of the Mysteries and Initiations on Earth', and also 'a temple of initiation where men rose towards the Gods and the Gods descended towards men'. She believed that the sarcophagus in the King's Chamber was actually a kind of baptismal font, and that the person to be initiated would be ritually laid out in it to undergo transformative experiences.

With such impressive credentials, it is no surprise that, for the well-travelled sorcerer, mage and quester after truth of the late nineteenth and early twentieth centuries, a trip to the Great Pyramid became as essential a component of a full life as it is for a certain brand of New Age tourist today. For some, of course, the trip was carried out purely on the astral plane, bypassing the services of Thomas Cook; but the list of those who went there in person is striking enough.

Peter Demianovich Ouspensky (1878–1947), the Russian mathematician-philosopher, sometime disciple of the strange and (in some ways) impressive Armenian mystic Gurdjieff, and, later, cult leader in his own right, went to the Pyramid on the eve of World War I. In *A New Model of the Universe* (1934), he wrote of his experiences in terms which, although hushed and reverent, do not greatly stretch the boundaries of likelihood: 'The incomprehensible past became the present and felt quite close to me, as if I could stretch out my arm into it, and our present disappeared and became strange, alien and distant ....'

A rather more lively account of such a jaunt can be found in the *Confessions* of Aleister Crowley (1875–1947), the self-styled *to mega therion* or Great Beast 666, known to the British yellow press as 'the wickedest man in the world' and certainly the most notorious of all twentieth-century practitioners of magic (or, as he spelled it, Magick). Crowley's name is still one much conjured with, sometimes literally, in Satanist circles, but his thrillingly evil reputation should not blind one to the fact that he was also an inveterate prankster and teller of tall tales.

Crowley claims that he spent one of his honeymoon nights in the King's Chamber of the Pyramid, reading out strange hermetic incantations by the light of a candle. Gradually, he says, he noticed that the walls began to glow with an unearthly light, and soon the whole chamber was bright enough for him to carry on reading without needing his candle. A few days later his bride appears to have had a mystical encounter with an Egyptian deity, but that is another (tall) story.

The most detailed and colourful contribution to the my-night-in-the-Pyramid genre can be found in a book which was, in its day, a considerable best-seller:

A Search in Secret Egypt (1935) by 'Dr' Paul Brunton. Unlike Crowley, Brunton was not a trickster: he expected to be taken quite seriously, and often was. Later in life he cultivated many disciples, who supported him financially and took his advice on everything from sexual intercourse (abstain from it) to real estate (buy heavily in South America so as to be safe from the nuclear war of the mid-1970s). An entertaining, exasperating and moving account of Brunton's later exploits can be found in a book by Jeffrey Masson with the self-explanatory title *My Father's Guru* (1993).

Although Brunton was not a cynical man, nor exploitative in any crass way, Masson recalls, he loved to cultivate an air of imponderably deep mystery about himself, usually by hints and cryptic smiles rather than blatant assertion. He liked, for example, to give the impression that he was a visitor from another planet, once calmly informing the young Masson that the reason he did not drive was that there were no cars on Venus. When

Aleister Crowley, self-styled Great Beast 666, claimed to have spent one of his honeymoon nights in the King's Chamber.

Masson grew older and more sceptical, he challenged Brunton about the nature of his much-flaunted doctorate. Brunton eventually conceded that it had been awarded by Roosevelt University in Chicago – an institution which, Masson later discovered, has no records for him. At other times, he would murmur that his true higher education had been conducted at the Astral University, located somewhere in the far reaches of the cosmos.

Meanwhile, back in Egypt, Brunton's famous Pyramid night went, he said, something like this: a sense of physical cold, followed by the psychic impression that the Chamber was 'peopled with unseen beings'. Then fear: 'There was something abroad which I sensed as evil, dangerous. A nameless dread flickered into my heart ....' Then pure panic, followed by a sort of Temptation of Saint Anthony: 'Monstrous elemental creations, evil horrors of the underworld, forms of grotesque, insane, uncouth and fiendish aspect gathered round me and afflicted me with unimaginable repulsion.' But a better class of apparition soon showed up. A couple of tall, wise figures, recognizable to the erudite Brunton as wearing 'the unmistakable regalia' of Egyptian high priests, came to him and asked: 'Why dost thou come to this place, seeking to evoke the secret powers? Are not mortal ways enough for thee?'

The apparitions then tried to get rid of Brunton with a few veiled threats, but, stout fellow, he would have none of it. Next, one of the duo ('I dared place no guess of years upon him') took him, put him into the sarcophagus and induced a trance-like state bordering on death. (Had the priest been reading his Madame Blavatsky? Or had Brunton?) As connoisseurs of such stories may by now have guessed, Brunton then had an out-of-body experience, rapidly followed by reunions with departed loved ones. Finally, the priest returned, told Brunton a thing or two about the universe and instructed him to 'Take back with thee the warning that when men forsake their creator and look on their fellows with hate, as with the princes of Atlantis in whose time this Pyramid was built, they are destroyed by the weight of their own iniquity, even as the people of Atlantis were destroyed ....' Various other oddities happened to Brunton after this dark threat, including a bit of a tease with secret chambers ('The mystery of the Great Pyramid is the mystery of thine own self. The secret chambers and ancient records are all contained in thine own nature ...'). And then he woke up. Astonishingly, his watch showed him that it was 'precisely the melodramatic hour of midnight, both hands pointing to twelve, neither more nor less!' – just as if the whole thing had been scripted by a hack writer of ghost stories. Brunton makes more Egyptian revelations, but it would be impolite to ignore the hint dropped by his high priest and we should now move on.

THE ATLANTEANS

The story of the mythical island continent of Atlantis has been told and retold many times, and all the more often since Plato wrote down his version in his two dialogues, the *Timaeus* and the *Critias*; like Dr Brunton's priestly friend, he asserted that the island sank beneath the waves as a result of its inhabitants' decadence. The definitive modern version of the Atlantis fad, however, can be attributed not to Plato but to an all-but-forgotten American author, Ignatius Donnelly (1831–1901), whose enormous best-seller *Atlantis* (1882) fired the imaginations of readers on both sides of the Atlantic. They included no less eminent a Victorian than the then Prime Minister, W. E. Gladstone, who was strongly tempted by the idea of raising an expedition to discover the sunken remains – squarely located by Donnelly in the mid-Atlantic.

Thanks to Donnelly – who was also an advocate of the crackpot theory that Shakespeare's plays were written by Francis Bacon – Atlantis has been lodged firmly in the popular imagination ever since. Some of his lesser contentions have proved equally tenacious, such as the view that the gods of just about every known civilization from Greece to India were actually the kings and queens of Atlantis in imperfectly remembered forms, and that Atlanteans colonized places as far afield as Scandinavia, South America ... and Egypt. Great chunks of Donnelly's work, unattributed, have been discovered in Madame Blavatsky's *Secret Doctrine*. Dreadful cynics might wish to follow the link from Donnelly to Blavatsky, from Blavatsky to Brunton, from Brunton ....

That would, at least, be one of the ways in which the link between Egypt and Atlantis wormed its way into modern myth. The other route can be traced back to a man who, again, is now little known outside occultist and related circles, but remains an enduring force within them: Edgar Cayce (1877–1945). Between 1901 and his death, the poorly educated Cayce regularly went into trance states in which he would advise his attentive listeners of many things – often medical matters, but he encompassed grander themes, too.

From about 1923 onwards, one of the items of 'information' Cayce would often tell his listeners was that they had lived previous lives in – where else? –

Edgar Cayce believed that Atlantean builders of the Great Pyramid had left behind a Hall of Records crammed with secrets.

Opposite, top
Ignatius Donnelly's *Atlantis*, first published in 1882.

Opposite, bottom
Erich Von Däniken's *Chariots of the Gods?*, a best-seller since 1969.

Atlantis. (Note that even by 1901, when Cayce began, Donnelly's book had been in circulation for almost twenty years.) He himself, it seems, had been an Atlantean priest in his time – he went by the name of Ra-Ta. About 20 per cent of Cayce's 14,246 readings concerned Atlantis. The most influential of his tales was that the more enlightened Atlantean citizens had fled the coming deluge and set up home in Egypt around 10,500 BC. Whatever the archeologists might have said, Cayce maintained that the Great Pyramid was built – or, at the very least, designed and laid out – *c.* 10,400 BC. The Atlanteans, he continued, had also left a Hall of Records, possibly in the Pyramid itself or very close by, crammed with their most marvellous secrets, which would be uncovered in the last twenty years of the millennium.

Now, unless someone at Giza is keeping very quiet indeed, Cayce seems to have shot wide of the mark. If his Hall of Records has not yet been located, it has not been for the want of trying. A surprising number of otherwise sane people continue to take Cayce and his prophecies seriously, undaunted even by the sobering fact that his Atlantean readings began only after he met Arthur Lammers, a wealthy amateur reader of Theosophical texts, which included those of Mme Blavatsky. Fringe Egyptological circles were abuzz in the late 1990s, expecting at any moment the announcement that Cayce's Hall of Records had finally been found. None came.

THE EXTRA-TERRESTRIALS

The reputation and principal idea of Erich Von Däniken (b. 1935), the Swiss hotelier turned radical archaeologist, are well known. His book *Chariots of the Gods?* was first published in English in 1969 and is still in print after many editions. It has been so popular that its main contentions are known even to those who have never read a word of his highly idiosyncratic prose. Essentially, Von Däniken has adapted the nineteenth-century idea that a higher civilization once populated the world at a time when our species was still primitive, that its records are preserved in the world's oldest monuments, and that our collective mythologies are a record of actual events, with Atlantean figures remembered as Gods. All Von Däniken did was to give the old story a twist suitable for the space-age 1960s. For Atlanteans, read visitors from other planets or galaxies.

There is little point, and not very much fun, in addressing Von Däniken's arguments, such as they are. (Although it is worth mentioning his interesting estimate that the Pyramid would have taken at least 664 years to build, using available Old Kingdom technology.) Although it is sometimes hard to make out precisely what Von Däniken is claiming and what he is merely playing with, at the heart of his Egyptology appears to be the claim that the Great Pyramid was a sort of freezing chamber, where the significant dead could be preserved until Ra – an extra-terrestrial astronaut – came back from the heavens to revive them; and that it was built with the help of laser beams and helicopters. Von Däniken has made a great deal of money from his books and others have followed his lead.

PYRAMID POWER

In the 1960s and early 1970s there was a short-lived fad which attributed miraculous powers not only to Khufu's Pyramid but to anything made in a similar shape, no matter its scale or substance – cardboard, paper or plastic would do just as well as limestone and granite. The craze seems to have originated in the 1920s, when a Frenchman, Antoine Bovis, visited the Great Pyramid and noticed that there were dustbins in the King's Chamber (how did they get there?) containing dead cats (how did they get there?) which, instead of decaying in the humid air, had inexplicably mummified. He went home and built himself a wooden scale model of the Pyramid, 3 feet (1 metre) high, and placed a convenient dead cat beneath it. Sure enough, it mummified, as did other organic matter he placed there.

In the 1960s Karel Drbal, a Czech radio engineer, read reports of these antics and made a few experiments of his own. He claimed that a used razor blade, placed underneath a cardboard pyramid just 6 inches (15 cm) high, would be restored to its original sharpness, and that this enabled him to shave some two hundred times using the same standard razor blade without undue pain or bleeding. Delighted, he took out a patent on his 'Cheops Pyramid Razorblade Sharpener', making them first of cardboard and then from Styrofoam. Elsewhere in Europe, reports reached the press of small pyramids being used to keep yoghurt and milk fresh without refrigeration.

Diagram of Karel Drbal's 'Cheops Pyramid Razorblade Sharpener'.

RECENT PYRAMIDOLOGY

To bring this survey up to date, let us conclude with a summary of some of the things that have been said of the pyramids in the last couple of decades or so, generally in books that have sold extremely well.

The extra-terrestrial theme has been pursued in a series of popular books with the collective title *The Earth Chronicles*, by Zecharia Sitchin, including *The Twelfth Planet* (1976), *The Stairway to Heaven* (1980) and *The Wars of Gods and Men* (1985). Using ancient Mesopotamian texts as his authority, Sitchin contends that the human race was created by a form of genetic engineering, and is in fact the brainchild of a race known as the Anunnaki, inhabitants of an undiscovered planet in our own solar system.

Sitchin maintains that the Great Pyramid was a key component in a kind of large-scale spaceport runway for the flying craft of the Anunnaki, who apparently favoured Baalbeck in the Lebanon as their regular landing site. (Sitchin, incidentally, is one among many non-orthodox writers who believe that Howard Vyse faked the hieroglyphic graffiti in the spaces above the King's Chamber.)

Yet another variant on the ET theme looks not to an unknown planet but to our familiar neighbour Mars, and specifically to the shape photographed by the American space probe *Viking II* in 1976, which to some looks like a humanoid

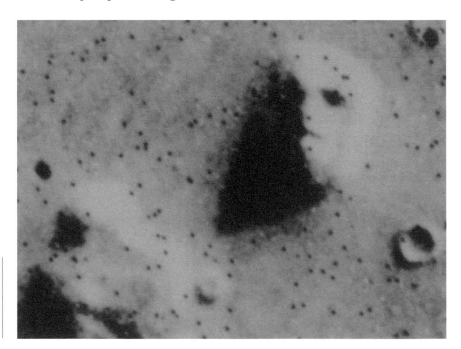

The so-called 'Face on Mars' rock formation photographed by the American space probe *Viking II* in 1976, in which some people have seen the likeness of the Giza Sphinx.

face and to others like a group of random shadows on rock. Various electronic tinkerings with the so-called 'Face on Mars' pictures have accentuated its similarity to the face of the Sphinx, leading some observers to the not immediately self-evident conclusion that the Sphinx was actually carved by émigré Martians, fleeing an imminent comet impact some 12,000 years ago. One of the principal advocates of this case is Richard Hoagland, a former NASA consultant.

The presence of such ET themes in popular fiction and films should not be overlooked. Highly successful movies such as *Stargate* and *The Fifth Element* take for granted a kind of diffuse modern folklore linking ancient Egypt to the distant reaches of the cosmos, while at least one recent science-fiction novelist has played with the idea that the pyramids were used as a huge protective shield for sorcerers who had found a way to tap the energy of the Van Allen belts (regions of intense radiation partly surrounding the Earth), channelling it down through the earth's atmosphere to the tip of the Great Pyramid itself.

The 'ancient knowledge' theme has developed quite a few interesting new variations of late. One, which can be found in the work of Alan Alford (*Gods of the New Millennium*, 1997; *The Phoenix Solution*, 1998) echoes both New Age and science fiction ideas by proposing that the Pyramid was, among other functions, a giant energy generator. Much the same line of argument may be found in Christopher Dunn's *The Giza Power Plant* (1998). Andrew Collins – the author of *From the Ashes of Angels* (1997) and *Gods of Eden* (1998) – and others have put forward the related suggestion that the Egyptians may have known how to levitate large stone blocks, possibly by the use of sound. This 'sonic' theme probably has a lot of mileage left in it.

Another widely circulated proposition returns to the theme of superior astronomical knowledge. In *The Orion Mystery* (1995), Robert Bauval and Adrian Gilbert contend that the three Giza pyramids were laid out to reflect the three main stars in the 'belt' of the constellation of Orion. As fringe theories go, this was relatively modest, and the authors, although doubtless aware of the huge potential readership for the ancient mystery genre, were careful not to attribute any of their observations to magic or aliens. (However, rationalists will have noted that another of Gilbert's publications is entitled *The Cosmic Wisdom Beyond Astrology*, and that he is the founder of Solos Press, which specializes in 'Christian Mysticism, Gnosticism and the Hermetic Tradition of Egypt'. Moreover, among the authorities acknowledged in his books is one Erich Von Däniken.)

Gilbert and Bauval have since given up their collaboration, but the latter went on to write *Keeper of Genesis* (1997), with the well-known 'alternative'

historian of ancient civilizations, Graham Hancock. More recently, their *Mars Mystery* (1998) looked at the 'Face-on-Mars' notions of Hoagland and others.

Finally, for as long as the so-called 'door' in the shaft running up from the Queen's Chamber remains unopened (see Chapter 4), there will be plenty of people confident that it leads to an unknown chamber, containing all manner of mysteries.

The popular appetite for fringe beliefs about the pyramids seems all but insatiable. A longer discussion would have to take in work by writers who cannot be dismissed as readily as Von Däniken, and whose work currently occupies a curious position, well outside standard academic orthodoxy but at some distance from the airport book stands.

For example, the substantial body of work by Schwaller de Lubicz, a genuinely erudite, if maverick, scholar. His books, mainly in French, though now being translated into English, resume the now-familiar theme that, as his exponent John West puts it, 'Egyptian science, medicine, mathematics and astronomy were all of an exponentially higher order of refinement and sophistication than modern scholars will acknowledge.'

Then there are two notable defectors from the straight academic world to the shadows of 'pyramidology': Livio Catullo Stecchini and Giorgio de Santillana. The latter is a renowned historian of Renaissance science and author of a major book on Galileo. Despite his authority, de Santillana could not find an academic publisher for *Hamlet's Mill: An Essay in Myth and the Frame of Time* (1969), which he wrote in collaboration with H. Von Dechend. The academic verdict on such books has generally been either damning or sublimely indifferent, but it is likely that they will continue to influence the wilder fringes of non-professional Egyptology for a long time to come.

Having given so much airing to the mystics, the occultists, the prophets and the connoisseurs of extra-terrestrial life, it seems fitting to hand over the final verdict on pyramidology to the acknowledged father of modern Egyptology, Flinders Petrie, who in his memoir *Seventy Years in Archaeology* wrote: 'It is useless to state the real truth of the matter, as it has no effect on those who are subject to this type of hallucination. They can be left with the flat earth believers, and other such people to whom a theory is dearer than fact.'

Opposite
In *The Orion Mystery* (1995), Robert Bauval and Adrian Gilbert contend that the Giza pyramids were laid out to reflect the three main stars in the 'belt' of the Orion constellation, which they very nearly do. The stars, from top to bottom, are: *Mintaka* (Menkaure's pyramid), *Al Nilam* (Khafre's pyramid) and *Al Nitak* (Khufu's pyramid).

GLOSSARY

akh Supernatural state of being, sometimes translated as 'Spirit of Life' or 'Transfigured One'. Once a dead person's *ka* and *ba* had been reunited, his spirit could occupy its place in the heavens in the divine form of an *akh*. *See ba, ka* and pages 104–6.

akhet Ancient Egyptian season running from mid-July to mid-November, literally 'inundation'. The hottest time of the year, when the rains fell and the Nile overflowed.

Anubis Egyptian deity. Jackal-headed god of embalming, weigher of hearts and ruler of the realm of the dead, west of the Nile.

Atum Egyptian deity. The creator of space and time, from whose tears mankind and the gods were made. Also worshipped as the evening manifestation of the sun-god.

auroura Egyptian unit of area equal to 47 square yards (about 40 square metres).

ba Supernatural element of the ancient Egyptian afterlife. It is sometimes represented as a large bird with a human head, charged with the task of searching for the departed *ka*. *See akh, ka* and pages 104–6.

bay Straight palm rib with a V-shaped slot in one end used either as a solar clock by day or an astral clock at night. Sometimes used in conjunction with a *merkhet* at alignment ceremonies.

Bes Egyptian deity. Protective god of birth and sexuality with powers against disease and danger.

'Bringing the Foot' Funeral ritual in which the burial chamber was ceremonially brushed clean and libations offered.

canopic vessels Sealed containers, often jars, designed to hold the embalmed entrails of a deceased person removed during mummification and entombed with them for use in the afterlife.

Cheops Greek name for Khufu.

'Coming Forth at the Voice' Funeral ritual, possibly involving animal sacrifice, in which a dead king was invited to enjoy the offerings of his tomb.

cubit Unit of length equal to about 21 inches (52.5 cm) and divided into seven hands of four fingers each. Based on the length of the forearm from the elbow to the tip of the middle finger.

decan The Egyptian ten-day week: nine days of work and one of rest.

Djedefre (2528–2520 BC) Khufu's short-reigning son and successor.

Djoser (2630–2611 BC) IIIrd Dynasty king during whose reign the first step pyramid was built.

ëspn Drug, possibly extracted from poppies, used to pacify babies.

faience Glazed clay or steatite overlaid with coloured glass.

Gate of the Crow Towering entrance to the workers' city of the Giza plateau.

Geb Egyptian deity. God of the earth. Son of Shu and Tefnut and brother of Nut.

Gerget Khufu Settlement populated by those who served the Pyramid complex.

Hathor Egyptian deity. Protector goddess of love and maternity, birth and regeneration. Depicted as a cow or in human form bearing a solar disk between the horns of a cow. Consort of Horus.

Hemiunu Khufu's younger brother, who was charged with overseeing the construction of the Great Pyramid.

Her-Mejedu Khufu's Horus name.

Hetepheres Mother of Khufu.

hieroglyphs Ideographic and phonetic picture signs used to write the ancient Egyptian language. *See* pages 137–40.

Horus Name (literally, 'the distant one') used to designate a number of Egyptian sky-gods and gods of kingship who took the form of a hawk. In Osirian theology, the son of Isis and Osiris.

Ibu en Waab Tent of Purification, where a dead body was purified before entering the tomb.

intermediate periods The three relatively short periods in Egyptian history when the country was divided and ruled simultaneously by a number of kings. The first intermediate period lasted from the beginning of the VIIth to the end of the Xth Dynasty (2181-2040 BC); the second from the beginning of the XIVth to the end of the XVIIth Dynasty (1640-1550 BC); and the third from the beginning of the XXIst to the end of the XXIVth Dynasty (1070-712 BC).

Invocation Offering *see* 'Coming Forth at the Voice'.

Imhotep Djoser's Chancellor and High Priest of the sun-god Re, responsible for designing and building the first step pyramid.

Isis Egyptian deity. The greatest of goddesses, wife of Osiris, mother of Horus and goddess of the dead. Venerated as a mother, she is usually depicted in human form with her head surmounted by a throne (the hieroglyph of her name), or by the horns of a cow and a solar disk.

ka Supernatural element of the ancient Egyptian afterlife. Often translated as 'soul', 'spirit' or 'life-force', the concept defies translation. At the point of death the *ka* departs the body and was sometimes represented as a pair of raised arms, bent at the elbow, borne by a pair of running legs. *See akh, ba* and pages 104-6.

ka **servants** Caste of priests contracted by a person during their lifetime and charged with ensuring the continuity and propriety temple rituals after their death.

ka **statue** Statue entombed with the deceased that could provide a substitute for a dead person in the afterlife, should some harm come to their embalmed body. The statue usually resembled the deceased in youth and bore the *ka* symbol (two raised arms, bent at the elbow) on its head.

Khafre (also known as Chephren, 2520-2494 BC) Son of Khufu, for whom the second pyramid on the Giza plateau was built.

Khepri The cosmic scarab beetle, believed to push the sun over the horizon at dawn.

Khufu (also known as Cheops, 2551-2528 BC) Second king of the IVth Dynasty, for whom the Great Pyramid at Giza was built.

Kite Leader of a funeral procession – either the widow of a dead man or a professional mourner.

kohl Black powder derived from galena (lead ore) and used as eye-liner.

Lector Priest Priest who, at a funeral, read from a scroll of magical utterances and was thereby charged with the task of spiritually transforming the deceased into an *akh*.

maat Complex notion encompassing individual morality and creativity, social culture and justice, the physical structure of the universe and its deep underlying logic and equilibrium. Egyptians believed that a person's conduct in the present life – their adherence to *maat* – affected their wellbeing in the afterlife. Personified as the goddess Maat.

mastaba Raised, rectangular tomb structure of mudbricks or stones with sloping sides, usually above a subterranean chamber.

Menkaure (also known as Mycerinus, 2490-2472 BC) Grandson of Khufu, for whom the third pyramid on the Giza plateau was built.

merkhet Literally, an 'instrument of knowing' – a plumb line attached to a horizontal bar used in foundation ceremonies.

Middle Kingdom Period made up of the XIth, XIIth and XIIIth Dynasties (2040-1640 BC).

natron Naturally occurring substance containing sodium carbonate and sodium bicarbonate. It was mined in Lower Egypt and used to dry the corpse during mummification.

Nephthys Egyptian deity. Sister of Osiris, Seth and Isis. With Isis, she protected and revived the dead.

New Kingdom Period made up of the XVIIIth, XIXth and XXth Dynasties (1550-1070 BC).

Nut Egyptian deity. The sky goddess who presides over the realm of the stars.

Old Kingdom Period made up of the IIIrd, IVth, Vth and VIth Dynasties (2686-2181 BC).

'Opening of the Mouth' Magical funeral ritual involving spoken spells which, it was believed, would enable a dead king the breathe, eat and speak in the afterlife.

Osiris Egyptian deity. Mummiform judge of the dead, associated with order and harmony. Killed by Seth, he was revived in the afterlife by Isis and Nephthys, His successor, Horus, continued to do battle with Seth in this world.

peret Ancient Egyptian season running from mid-November to mid-March. Literally, 'emergence'; when the flood waters drained from the fields and the land became workable.

phyle Literally, 'tribe' – the Greek translation of *zaa*, a team of two hundred workers. It has been calculated that ten such teams made up the crew of workers that built the Great Pyramid.

Ptah Egyptian deity. Creator god of Memphis.

pyramidion The capstone of a pyramid.

Re Egyptian deity. Falcon-headed sun-god with whom rulers from the middle of the IVth Dynasty onwards were held to have a special relationship as 'Sons of Re'.

sarcophagus Outer container in which a coffin and mummy were placed. (Literally 'flesh-eater' in Greek.)

serdab A chamber inside a tomb that contained the deceased's body and *ka* statue. (Literally, 'cellar' in Arabic.)

Seshet Egyptian deity. Feminine counterpart of Thoth.

Seth Egyptian deity. The wild and chaotic desert god associated with evil, storms and bad weather. Murderer of Osiris and adversary of his successor, Horus.

shemu Ancient Egyptian season running from mid-March to mid-July. Literally, 'dryness'; when the Nile sank to its lowest level and the land became completely dry.

Shu Egyptian deity. God of the air, occupying the space between heaven and earth. Son of Atum and brother of Tefnut.

sinw A doctor.

Sneferu (2575-2551 BC) First king of the IVth Dynasty and father of Khufu.

Tawaret Egyptian deity. Goddess of fertility.

Tefnut Egyptian deity. Goddess of moisture. Daughter of Atum. Sister of Shu and mother of Geb and Nut.

Thoth Egyptian deity. Ibis-headed or baboon-shaped god of writing and measurement who records the verdicts of Osiris.

usekh Collar made of several rows of cylindrical beads in blue and green faience. A major fashion of the Old Kingdom.

ushabtis Miniature worker figures buried with the dead in the Middle Kingdom to enable the deceased to answer the gods' call to work in the afterlife. (The Egyptian for 'answer' is *usheb*.)

Wabet Literally 'pure', but usually translated as 'mortuary workshop'; a building where funeral rituals, including partial dismemberment of the corpse, took place.

Wet Literally, 'the Wrapper' – the chief embalmer, also known as the Seal-bearer of God, responsible for transforming a person's mortal remains into a mummy.

zaa A two hundred strong team of workers. *See phyle*.

Opposite
An early photograph of Arab guides helping tourists to climb the Great Pyramid in 1850.

FURTHER READING

THE TWO INDISPENSABLE WORKS on Egyptian pyramids are Mark Lehner's *The Complete Pyramids* (Thames & Hudson, 1997) and I. E. S. Edwards's *The Pyramids of Egypt* (Penguin, revised edition 1993). At the time of writing (2002), these are the most authoritative and complete studies suitable for the general reader.

The following general books on ancient Egypt are recommended: Cyril Aldred, *The Egyptians* (Thames & Hudson, 3rd edition, 1998); Guilemette Andreu, *Egypt in the Age of the Pyramids* (John Murray, 1997); J. Baines and J. Malek, *Atlas of Ancient Egypt* (Oxford, 1980); A. H. Gardiner, *Egypt of the Pharaohs* (Oxford, 1961); T. G. H. James, *An Introduction to Ancient Egypt* (British Museum, 1979); Manfred Lurker, *The Gods and Symbols of Ancient Egypt* (Thames & Hudson, 1982); Margaret A. Murray, *The Splendour that was Egypt* (Sidgwick & Jackson, 1963); Boris de Rachewiltz, *An Introduction to Egyptian Art* (Spring Books, 1966); W. Stevenson Smith, *The Art and Architecture of Ancient Egypt* (Penguin, revised edition 1965).

For those wishing to investigate the mysteries of the Egyptian language, the best primer is *How to Read Egyptian Hieroglyphs* (British Museum, 1998) by Mark Collier and Bill Manley.

The literature on the European rediscovery of Egypt is enormous. A good point of departure is Herodotus; *The Histories* is most readily available as a Penguin Classic, translated by Aubrey de Selincourt and A. R. Burn (1972). Concise overviews are provided by L. Greener's *The Discovery of Egypt* (Hippocrene Books, 1966), T. G. H. James's *Excavating in Egypt* (British Museum, 1982) and, with something of a French bias, Jean Vercoutter's small but lively picture book *The Search for Ancient Egypt*, translated by Ruth Sharman (Thames & Hudson, 1992). Flaubert's adventures are entertainingly preserved in *Flaubert in Egypt*, translated and edited by Francis Steegmuller (Penguin, 1996). A new edition of Sir Flinders Petrie's *The Pyramids and Temples of Gizeh* (originally published in 1883) is promised by Kegan Paul International in 2002 and good libraries will stock earlier editions, his autobiography and other popular books on Egyptian archaeology. Although derided by orthodox scholars, the first volume of Martin Bernal's *Black Athena: The Afroasiatic Roots of Classical Civilization* (Free Association, 1987) is a passionate and fascinating work, well worth reading if only for the disagreements it provokes. Finally – and despite its apparent distance from the subject of the pyramids – Christopher Frayling's *The Face of Tutankhamun* (Faber, 1992), includes some enjoyably sceptical accounts of various Egyptian crazes of the twentieth century, including Peter Green's witty essay 'The Treasures of Egypt'.

A remarkably sane and literate survey of pyramidology and fringe theories from the seventeenth century to the 1960s is provided by Peter Tomkins in *Secrets of the Great Pyramid* (Penguin, 1973). A more recent book, *Giza: The Truth* by Ian Lawton and Chris Ogilvie-Herald (Virgin Books, 2000), offers a reasonably calm account of present-day fringe theories, fantasies and manias, with particular reference to the best-sellers of Robert Bauval, Graham Hancock and others.

Beyond this point, we are in murky waters. Those with a ferocious appetite for theosophical mysteries may browse at their will in the likes of Madame Blavatsky's *Isis Unveiled* and *The Secret Doctrine* (both of which were published in new editions by the Theosophical University Press in 1984). Other mystic commentaries and polemics include John Michell's *The View Over Atlantis* (Sago Press, 1969) and *City of Revelation* (Garnstone, 1972), John Anthony West's *The Serpent in the Sky* (HarperCollins, 1979), Paul Brunton's *Search in Secret Egypt* (Weiser Books, 1984), R. A. Schwaller de Lubicz's *The Temple of Man* (translated from the French by Deborah Lawlor, Inner Traditions International, 1999) and Peter Lemesurier's *The Great Pyramid Decoded* (Element Books, 1996).

INDEX

Page numbers in *italics* refer to illustrations

PICTURE CREDITS

BBC Worldwide would like to thank the following individuals and organizations for providing photographs and for permission to reproduce copyright material. While every effort has been made to trace and acknowledge copyright holders, we would like to apologize should there be any errors or omissions.

Pages 2-3 Giraudon/Bridgeman Art Library; 7 © Richard T. Howitz/CORBIS; 8 The Hulton Archive; 9 The National Portrait Gallery London/AKG London; 11 Mary Evans Picture Library; 14 The Egyptian Museum, Cairo/AKG London; 19 The Egyptian Museum, Cairo/Werner Forman Archive; 21 AKG London © Erich Lessing; 22 Ancient Art & Architecture Collection © J. Stevens; 23 NEMES/Alan Fildes; 25 Ancient Art & Architecture Collection © Ronald Sheridan; 32 The Kobal Collection; 34 Science Photo Library; 35, 36 Werner Forman Archive; 37 Ancient Art & Architecture Collection © Mary Jelliffe; 38-9 SCALA; 40 Werner Forman Archive; 41 AKG London © Erich Lessing; 43, 44 Metropolitan Museum of Art, New York/Werner Forman Archive; 45 Jon Bodsworth, GIZA VIEW; 46 The Egyptian Museum, Cairo/Werner Forman Archive; 47 SCALA; 50 Jon Bodsworth, GIZA VIEW; 62 Brooklyn Museum/AKG London; 71 Private Collection/Bridgeman Art Library; 74 Stapleton Collection/Bridgeman Art Library; 75 Jon Bodsworth, GIZA VIEW; 76 Ancient Art & Architecture Collection © J. Stevens; 77 The Hulton Archive; 79 Jon Bodsworth, GIZA VIEW; 80 The Hulton Archive; 81 Jon Bodsworth, GIZA VIEW; 83 Cheops Barque Museum/Werner Forman Archive; 86 © Barnabas Bosshart/CORBIS; 89 AKG London; 91 The British Museum; 93 Staatliche Museen zu Berlin – Preussischer Kulturbesitz Ägyptisches Museum und Papyrussammlung Inv. 14396; 95 The Egyptian Museum, Cairo/Giraudon/Bridgeman Art Library; 96 *above* Topham Picturepoint, *below* Preussischer Kulturbesitz Ägyptisches Museum/AKG London © Erich Lessing; 97 Egyptian Museum, Cairo/SCALA; 102 Werner Forman Archive; 103 *above* E. Strouhal, *below* Ancient Art & Architecture Collection © J. Beecham; 106 Werner Forman Archive; 109 San Marco, Venice/SCALA; 111 Museo Nazionale, Naples/SCALA; 113 The Fotomas Index; 114 AKG London; 116 Jon Bodsworth, GIZA VIEW; 119 Mary Evans Picture Library; 122, 123 in Joscelyn Godwin *Athanasius Kircher: A Renaissance Man and the Quest for Knowledge*, Thames & Hudson 1979; 124 in Peter Tompkins *Secrets of the Great Pyramid*, Allen Lane 1973; 125 The Fotomas Index; 126 The National Portrait Gallery, London; 128 *above* Charles Walker Photographic, *below* © W. Cody/CORBIS; 129 Musée des Beaux Arts, Valenciennes/Giraudon/Bridgeman Art Library; 130 © Archivio Iconographico, S.A./CORBIS; 131, 132 in Peter Tompkins *Secrets of the Great Pyramid*, Allen Lane 1973; 133 Musée des Beaux Arts, Caen/Giraudon/Bridgeman Art Library; 135 Collège de France/AKG London; 135 Bibliothèque Nationale/Bridgeman Art Library; 136 *above* The Fotomas Index, *below* © Bettmann/CORBIS; 137 Stapleton Collection/Bridgeman Art Library; 138 Private Collection/Bridgeman Art Library; 139 Ancient Art & Architecture Collection © R. Sheridan; 140, 141 in Peter Tompkins *Secrets of the Great Pyramid*, Allen Lane 1973; 143 *above* The National Portrait Gallery, *below* AKG London; 144 Private Collection, Paris/AKG London; 148 AKG London; 149 The Petrie Museum of Egyptian Archaeology, University College London; 152 The Royal Geographical Society, London/photo Miss H. M. Murdoch; 155 Courtesy *The Guardian* newspaper; 157 AKG London; 158 Index, Barcelona/Bridgeman Art Library; 159 Werner Forman Archive; 162 Science Photo Library; 164 in Peter Tompkins, *Secrets of the Great Pyramid*, Allen Lane 1973; 166 The Royal Society of Edinburgh; 168 Jon Bodsworth, GIZA VIEW; 170, 171, 173 Mary Evans Picture Library; 174 *above* The Fortean Picture Library, *below* Courtesy Souvenir Press; 175 Mary Evans Picture Library; 178 Science Photo Library/NASA; 180 Science Photo Library; 185 Private Collection/Bridgeman Art Library.

Computer graphics on pages 17, 26, 28, 31, 48, 49, 51, 52-3, 55, 57, 59 (both), 60-1, 65, 66-7, 69, 84-5, 99 and 104 © BBC; produced by Jordi Bares, Henrik Holmberg, John Mitchell, Chris Thomas, Kia Van Beers, Nick Webber and Adrian Wyer at MillTv (London). Stills from the *Pyramid* television programme reproduced on pages 100 and 101 © BBC.